No Contact:
How to Beat the Narcissist

By

H G Tudor

D1502092

No Contact:

How to Beat the Narcissist

By

HG Tudor

Published by Insight Books

1. Introduction

The concept of No Contact is widely regarded as the most effective way by which a victim can escape the influence and effects of a narcissist. This is entirely correct. No Contact is the killer blow against the narcissist. It is hard to implement and even harder to maintain but I am going to discuss and analyse the concept of No Contact from the narcissist's perspective which will give you a hitherto unseen look at how this principle works, how it affects my kind and most importantly of all it will provide you with the information and knowledge that will prove invaluable in your quest to beat the narcissist.

The starting point for understanding how best to implement and maintain No Contact is to understand what it is that the narcissist wants. Many people when asked this question will respond by suggesting things such as control, domination, superiority, attention, admiration, the destruction of those who oppose him and similar suggestions. All of those descriptions are correct but they happen to be by-products of the one thing that a narcissist wants. We want just one thing. The sole reason we engage with certain individuals is because they provide us with one thing; fuel. This fuel is the catchall for any form of emotional reaction whether it is through word or deed that another person provides to us. It may be an admiring look, attentive comments, angry insults, tear-filled pleading or a tender hug. All of these and far more amount to the provision of fuel. We need fuel. It is the very thing that secures our existence for reasons, which I have expanded on in the book **Fuel.** We require this fuel each and every day. This is why we invariably select a primary appliance to supply us with this fuel and then engage in creating fuel lines to lots of different alternative appliances (supplemental sources) to ensure we have a steady stream of fuel through our waking hours. The removal of this fuel is what we dread more than anything else. Puncture this supply or even worse cause its cessation and we are forced to take dramatic steps. Initially, we will strive to re-establish the provision of fuel by unleashing every manipulative device in our devilish toolkit but if the cessation continues we have no choice but to seek our fuel from an alternative source. We cannot be starved of this precious resource for too long. The consequence of this is not something that we wish to contemplate.

Accordingly, the institution of No Contact will bring about the cessation of the supply of fuel. We will fight to recover it, although amongst the lesser of our brethren this fight will be short-lived since the expenditure of energy involved in doing so will soon outweigh the potential gain. This, along with the fear of the consequence of being deprived of fuel for too long will force the lesser narcissist to seek out fuel from somewhere else. Thus, you will be freed from his or her grip. The greater narcissist will apply his or her manipulative wiles for a longer period, spurred on by the twin combination of the potentially ultra-sweet fuel that results from a successful Hoover and the desire to punish you for having the audacity to interrupt the supply of fuel in the first place. You will be subjected to a longer period as the greater narcissist fights hard to secure the supply once again and to lash out at you. Even when the lesser or greater narcissist has given up on the fuel returning any time soon they never truly go away. Should you ever allow them the opportunity; they will Hoover again in order to bring about the return of the fuel supply. The narcissist never vanishes. Instead, he or she sits like some dormant virus ready to spring into life when the conditions to do so are favourable. To this end, you must always be on guard to ensure you do not sail back into the narcissist's sphere of influence. In a later chapter I explain what you can expect in terms of duration and intensity of Hoovering from either a lesser or greater narcissist in differing scenarios.

Thus No Contact is the fatal blow against the narcissist. By going No Contact, you will deprive him or her of the precious fuel and eventually cause the

4

narcissist to leave you alone and seek fuel from some other source. You can never let your guard totally down but you will be able to live your life free of the toxic influence of the narcissist. No Contact is the stake through the heart of the vampire; it is the silver bullet that slays the werewolf and the kryptonite, which renders Superman just a man. No Contact is the thermonuclear weapon in the victim's arsenal and if used appropriately and most importantly, when maintained, it will allow near total freedom from the influence of the narcissist. Whilst it may be the silver bullet you of course need to know how to fire that bullet and where to aim otherwise this golden opportunity becomes a lost opportunity to rid yourself of the narcissist who plagues your life. No Contact is a very simple concept. It is the complete and utter cessation of all contact with the narcissist on every level and in every circumstance. It is a complete shutdown of communications. It is the eradication of the narcissist from every facet of your life and the rigid and unwavering commitment to never straying from such a course of action. It is all about staying away and keeping away. Simple enough concept you will agree, yet whilst the concept is straight forward, the execution of this doctrine is far more difficult.

This is for two reasons. Firstly, it is because of what you will do. Secondly, it is because of what we will do. By the time you have any realisation that you have been ensnared by a narcissist you may well have endured years, many years, of the push and pull, the cycle of seduction and devaluing, the discard and the Hoover. You are unlikely to have realised what has happened to you without outside help because our ways are so subtle and insidious that you have little hope or realisation on your own. You need others to smash the brick of awareness in your face in order to wrench you from the false reality that we have created and deposited you in. Once you have been given this awareness the period of abuse that you have been subjected to will have been substantial and significant. You will be exhausted, quite possibly having had a nervous breakdown. You will exhibit the symptoms of post-traumatic stress disorder your confidence will be shot, your self-esteem will be on the floor, your coping mechanisms eroded and your capability for critical thinking eradicated. You are left in an extremely vulnerable position. This makes you highly susceptible to the Hoover to draw you back into the dance with the narcissist. You cannot be blamed for falling for this overture once again. You have little in the way of defences and then you face the charm, the seduction and the promise of the golden period once again. Few can resist this in such a weakened state and accordingly they become sucked back into the narcissist's world once again. They enjoy a brief period of rejoicing as the narcissist rolls out the illusion that suckered the victim the first time around before the denigration and devaluation begins once again. This cycle will go round and round and round. Intelligent, independent, self-sufficient and strong people will fall for this seduction and the process of devaluation, discard and Hoover. There is no shame in admitting this because even the most socially adept, emotionally aware and intuitive individual can be and is ensnared by the narcissist. We are complete experts in the art of the seductive illusion. We have been created to seduce so we get our fuel. We have plenty of experience at luring people in with our sugarcoated words and empty promises and next to nobody can resist us. If you could not resist us at the very outset, before you became drained by us, what chance have you got when we apply such overtures when we have you in an exhausted and run-down state? Accordingly, the instigation of No Contact is very difficult for you because of the condition you find yourself in when you realise that you must deploy No Contact. Yet, your difficulties do not end there. Not only have you been stripped of the positive resources which would help you maintain No Contact you will be come under repeated and sustained attack from us as we seek to Hoover you. I will be detailing later in this book what you can expect to happen when you try and implement No Contact, the campaign that will be launched against you and the various Power Plays that will be deployed against you. Knowing that these are in the pipeline and how they will manifest will prove particularly valuable to you. You need to know how the narcissist will react once you make that decision to implement No Contact. You must know what is in store for you to allow yourself any chance of maintaining No Contact in a successful manner. Very few people implement No Contact in a successful manner the first time. There are four reasons for this.

Firstly, they are not sufficiently strong enough. Secondly, they are unprepared for just how dangerous the narcissist becomes when No Contact begins. Thirdly, they have not prepared their exit and make many elementary errors (I suggest you read **Departure Imminent: Preparing for No Contact to Beat the Narcissist** for further advice as you ready yourself for No Contact). The fourth reason is that the person seeking to implement No Contact has not read this book. This book is going to tell you all about how the narcissist regards No Contact, how we react to it, what we will do, what you must do and most of all it will allow you to see deep into the twisted and evil mind of the narcissist so you understand why things happen. As a victim of a narcissist you will have strong empathic qualities and one of those traits is the desire to know. Empaths always like to know why things happen. We, by contrast, have no interest in the whys. It is all about the outcome to us. We want to achieve the aim and we are not in the slightest bit interested as to why this happens so long as it does. The empathic individual on the other hand is committed to wanting to know, needing to understand and this often proves your downfall. The narcissist is not a creature of logic, or at least, not logic, as you know it. In our world we see everything as straight forward and making sense. This is not applicable to the way you regard things. We will say one thing and a moment later contradict ourselves. You will point this out to us and we will deny any such contradiction even going so far as to deny we even made the first statement. To you this is utterly illogical and you cannot comprehend how we cannot see what we have said or done. To us it is a necessary device, which allows us to maintain the upper hand with you. We assert our control over you and most importantly your perplexed reaction to this contradictory behaviour provides us with fuel. You do not realise this. You do not understand why this is the case and you keep striving (and we want you to keep doing this) to look for an answer which is grounded in the logic of your world. You will never achieve this. Instead all you will do is keep granting us power over you. You will keep giving us fuel. You will keep tying yourself in knots, exhausting yourself and becoming ground down as you try and work out why we do as we do. You make the same mistake every time. You try and analyse our behaviour through *your* viewpoint. This will not work. Once you learn to look at why we say what we say and do what we do, through *our* viewpoint all becomes clear. It will still seem illogical but you will at least understand.

That is the key to a successful implementation of No Contact. You must understand your foe before you can ever hope to defeat him. You need to work out why we act as we do, why we will take certain steps and in so understanding you maximise your prospects of executing and most importantly maintaining No Contact. This understanding can only come from one place; the mind of the narcissist. There are many who are fully familiar with the concept of No Contact because they know it works from the anecdotal evidence provided to them. The professionals and the therapists are well aware of how effective the concept of No Contact is. They will also have a rudimentary understanding as to why it is effective but they cannot tell you with any precision or detail just why it is effective in the way that the narcissist can. In the way that I can. There are plenty of victims (or survivors if they use that word instead) who have lived through an entanglement with the narcissist. The victim has experienced the dizzying seduction, the mesmerising golden period where they finally got to meet their soul mate. They were bombarded with love and affection and placed on that pedestal. They then experienced the incomprehensible and vicious devaluation as they found themselves hated and despised by the narcissist even though they had no understanding of why this was happening to them. They clung on desperately trying to establish why they were being treated in such an awful fashion. They hung on trying to return to the golden period before they were cast aside like a piece of rubbish. As they sat dazed and confused the narcissist Hoovered them up again and easily pulled them back into the false reality. The victim went willingly since he or she had no comprehension that this was but a further step along the road when one couples with a narcissist. This victim will have been pushed and pulled over many years and will have many battle stories about the war they fought with the narcissist. Certainly the recollections from a victim have value. They have earned their stripes and witnessed at first hand the seduction, the devaluation, the discard and the Hoover. They know the moves and can identify the red flags once they have been able to recover and view the whole torrid affair from a reasonable distance of objectivity. All of this puts them in a strong position to provide others with advice and there is admittedly considerable value in their recollections however they may still not understand why certain things happened. They will not have grasped why the narcissist behaved in certain ways and acted as he did. The victim can warn what to look for but the victim clearly does not know the narcissist inside out.

To gain a true understanding of how the narcissist reacts and regards No Contact there is only one source to go to and that is the narcissist himself. Only by grasping the nettle and reading how the narcissist will respond to the implementation of No Contact, what is he thinking, what he is planning and what he intends to do, will you truly be able to become fully informed and in so doing maximise your prospects of success. By reading this book you are being granted unrivalled access into the mind of the narcissist so that you can learn all about why we do as we do. It is not comfortable reading at times. It is likely to trigger unpleasant memories and experiences but I make no apology for that. I am not here to soften the blows since to do so would do you a dis-service. By reading what I have to write about the concept of No Contact you are engaging directly with me and on my terms. I am telling you exactly how it is and this is how it must be to enable you to get the most from this information. This is the way it must be done to enable you to understand. I will take you through what you will need to do to implement No Contact and most of all I will be detailing to you what you can expect your narcissist to do in response. How do I know all of this? Firstly, I am a narcissist. I have an awareness of who I am as a consequence of my intellect and also the ongoing treatment that I am involved in which has increased my insight. Secondly, I know all of this because I have had several victims attempt No Contact with me. In the same way that the victim has lived through the attempt to implement No Contact, I, as a narcissist have lived through being on the receiving end. I therefore have reacted to it, attacked it and defeated No Contact. I know how to shatter those defences. I know precisely what to do to ensure that No Contact does not work. I know so many deceitful and manipulative tricks that ensnare the unwary and pull them back into the nightmare. I have done this many times and thus I know just how effective these methods are. Thirdly, I know how your narcissist will respond because we are all similar in the way we behave. Yes, some of us are more malign and malevolent than others. Some of us will go further than others in our desire to secure fuel and to punish our victims. Some of us exhibit a greater degree of sadism in our behaviour. Some of us act with a totally focussed and driven manner but at the end of the day our behaviours are very similar. This is the case for one simple reason. They work. We all act in a similar way because we know that these are the methods that achieve our goals and as a consequence there is no need for us to act in a different manner. I have witnessed others of my brethren as they go about their seduction and denigration and allied with my heightened awareness I have observed the similarities. I have also been assisted by the information that the good doctors have relayed to me which adds to this library of information about how we behave. I have it mentioned countless times to me by those who interact with me through my social media outlets that they think that I am the narcissist in their life. These people are utterly convinced of it. They strive to establish that I am the person who has been plaguing them or continues to do so, but they are wrong. I do not know any of them and yet they still think I am their narcissist. The reason for this is that our behaviours are so strikingly similar. Thus, because of this, I am in a fantastic position to explain to you why we behave as we do and for it to be as applicable to me as it is to the narcissist that you are entangled with.

You have direct access to the workings of the narcissistic mind. This is a rare opportunity for you to understand why we act as we do and for all of this understanding to be applied to the concept of No Contact. I will address many facets of this doctrine, all from the perspective of the narcissist, which will give you a massive boost to your understanding and thus in turn a huge increase in your chances of successfully implementing No Contact.

You may be wondering why would a narcissist act in what seems to be a charitable manner by sharing these insights. Why would a narcissist help other people and give away his secrets? Surely this will make life harder for him if he forewarns people in this way? These are valid considerations, but, as I have explained in other publications, there are so many potential victims out there, no matter how widely read I might like this book to be, not everyone will avail themselves of the golden information contained within these pages. There will always be those who remain ignorant to our type and our wiles and thus there will always be plenty of victims for my type and me. My life will not be harder in any way for sharing this information. I do this not because I wish to help, but rather because I enjoy writing and this forms part of the terms of my treatment, which, for personal reasons, I am committed to seeing through. The dissemination of this information, in part arising from my increased awareness from my treatment, has become a condition of my treatment and accordingly you are in the fortunate position of being able to access it because I have to write it. Furthermore, I am a great believer in self-determination and by placing this information in your hands I am giving you that chance to determine your own fate. But most of all I do this because I like a challenge. The tussle I face with a determined empathic person who wishes to escape my clutches has me quivering with anticipation, not least at the prospect of the divine fuel that I will harvest following my successful conquering of my victims. If they are able to fight on a little longer because they have read this book, then I for one welcome it. The prospects of anyone I target having read this publication are likely to be low but if they have then it provides an added attraction to ensnare them and look to defeat their attempt to implement No Contact.

So dear reader prepare yourself for platinum-grade information from the narcissist himself as you learn all about how to implement No Contact and how we will seek to disrupt and destroy your attempt. I will take you through the necessity of understanding what No Contact really is, how easily it can actually be breached by you and what the consequences of such a breach are. I shall explain to you how No Contact is so effective in tackling us, giving you exactly how it feels for us to have it used against us. I will explain to you why No Contact is notoriously difficult to execute in order to enable you to see the pitfalls in advance and try to avoid them. I will detail the steps you must take to prepare for and maintain No Contact so your prospects of success are maximised. I will give you a blow-by-blow account of what happens from the moment you instigate No Contact and we become aware of that fact. I will take you through our response as we blitzkrieg you seeking to stun you into submission and then what follows. I will allow you to read about the various Power Plays we will deploy against you during the blitzkrieg and thereafter during No Contact if you are still able to maintain it. Knowing that these Power Plays are coming your way will arm you with treasured information and allow you to prepare to deal with them. I will explain how long you can expect the narcissist to keep trying to Hoover you and what will arise in the long-term should No Contact have lasted that long. All told this is the definitive resource for going No Contact and beating the narcissist.

HG Tudor

2. What is No Contact?

In order to enable you to implement No Contact in an effective fashion one of the things that you must be acquainted with is actually understanding what No Contact is. I cannot emphasise enough how you need to realise and understand what No Contact actually means. I will happily wager that by the time you finish this particular chapter you will have been surprised to learn what amounts to contact and how you would not have thought that such a step would be contact and moreover you had no idea what the consequences would be that flow from such a breach of the ideal of No Contact. You may think you have an idea of what No Contact is but believe me that you need to reconsider and re-appraise this concept if you are to try to defeat my kind. Grasping what No Contact amounts to and also understanding the ways in which it can be breached and the consequences which arise from that are a vital part of preparing you for the successful implementation of No Contact.

You may think that you already know what No Contact is. Surely it is having nothing to do with the particular narcissist who has sunk his or her claws into you? In short yes that is the concept but you need to know how that looks in reality. Remember, we are specialists at creating illusions and obscuring reality so that you may think you are looking at something when really it is something else. We apply this technique to obscure the concept of No Contact so that it becomes weakened and diluted. You think you are maintaining No Contact but subjected to our manipulative wiles you are actually eroding the concept and little by little allowing us to exert our influence over you again.

It is necessary for you to understand how No Contact appears in the real world because of the inherent vulnerability that we have imbued you with from the time you have been entangled with us. You will not realise this but part of our manipulation of you is to bury deep inside you that desire to always want us. No matter how much abuse we subjected you to, no matter how awful we behaved towards you and how horrible our treatment of you was, we engineer your emotions that you will still feel love for us. This happens for two reasons. The first is that our seduction of you is so overwhelmingly powerful and addictive you will always want to return to that state. You will, no matter how disgusting our treatment of you, want that golden period again and again. It is massively addictive and we deliberately made it this way. The second reason you will always feel love for us is because of whom you are. There are many reasons why we choose people like you; empathic people and this will be the subject of a forthcoming publication. We choose you because you provide fuel like nobody else. We choose you because your various traits of wanting to heal and fix keep you clinging on to us. Your desire to know and understand means you will not give up and you will hang on in there when others would fall by the wayside. We choose you because you will love and care for us, catering to the victim mentality that we narcissists all carry to a greater or lesser extent. There are many reasons why we choose you as our victims but one of the reasons, which is applicable to you always loving us, is that you, more than other types of people truly believe in the power of love. You are advocates of the concept of love conquering all, that love is all you need and that if you have love then everything else will be all right. You want to be in love. You want to give love and be loved. You are totally devoted to love in a way, which transcends other people. This devotion makes you highly susceptible to needing to love us. No matter what your head tells you, your emotions (the very things we want because of their fuel-giving qualities) will seek to override rational thought and you will want to be with us and experiencing the golden period. This desire is massively powerful. It will eradicate years of abuse such is its potency and we imbue this feeling in you through our application of the seduction and the golden period. By melding your capacity for loving with the highly addictive qualities of the golden period we create a potent mix, which is embedded deep inside of you. It

15

is always there ready to be activated. It is dormant, sleeping and doing nothing for long periods of time but it is most certainly there. We have created this mixture and left it within you ready to be activated. How is it activated? By us. The slightest of contact with us, no matter in what form, awakens this potent mixture and it starts to spread through you. The memories attached to it come flooding back and you experience all those wonderful and heightened emotions. Your mind is screaming at you to remember how badly we treated you, how miserable you felt and how you were left in a pit of despair but you pay those warning thoughts no heed. The mixture is so strong and all it takes is the slightest form of contact with us (whether that is direct or indirect) and the mixture is awakened to flood through you. It becomes all the more difficult to resist because the way this mixture has been formulated is to make you want to see more of us because this will increase the mixture's potency. Like any drug that is no good for you, it is highly addictive and unleashes powerful and wonderful feelings that are do difficult to resist. Accordingly, a combination of our addictive loving of you and your dedication to love combines to create this devastating mixture. This mixture sits inside of you having been placed there by us and we know that establishing some form of contact with you will trigger the activation of the mixture so you will want to be with us.

It is the activation of this mixture that you are fighting against when you seek to implement No Contact. It is like a highly flammable substance, which if brought near to an increase in heat, not even a naked flame, will ignite and explode. That is how powerful it is and how easy it is for it to be activated. It is set on a hair trigger and all it takes is for there to be some form of contact with us. Accordingly, in order to avoid this activation, you need to be aware of what No Contact really means. If you do not grasp this concept and moreover how it appears in the real world you run the repeated risk of allowing the ignition of the mixture and thereafter being susceptible to its influence over, you so that you are drawn back into our world.

This mixture is designed by us and is a purposeful act on our part. Like a bomb waiting to be set off, we leave it with you, content in the knowledge that all we need do is establish the merest form of contact and then the mixture is activated and your willpower to stay away from us will be severely tested. In some people they cave in immediately. The heady sensations that are awoken by the activation of the mixture prove too hard to resist and especially so for someone who is heart-broken and in a despairing condition. The arrival of the pleasure, the happy memories and those wonderful sensations that come with the activation of the mixture are difficult to resist for the most determined person. Someone who has been stripped of their self-esteem, browbeaten and beaten down is virtually unable to do anything about resisting the lure of the mixture and the resumption of their involvement with the narcissist. It is because of the creation and placement of this mixture that No Contact must be implemented. It is the only way to defeat the activation of the mixture. The more contact occurs the greater the ignition of the mixture and the subsequent severe difficulties in resisting its effect.

Unfortunately for you, you will never be able to completely eradicate me from you because of the existence of the mixture. I have achieved this absolutely on purpose. I have shattered your being and your heart and you will repair most of it. You will eventually conquer the shame at being hoodwinked. You will restore your finances and your broken home. You will reduce and extinguish the anxiety and trauma you felt. It will take a long time. It will take effort and discipline but you will get there. You will however not be able to repair your heart entirely. There will always be a small crack, a hairline fracture, and a slight puncture hole in it. That is the permanent effect of having danced with me. I know that crack is there and if ever given the chance I will activate the mixture so it creeps through that crack, seeps through the fracture and trickles into the hole. From there, it will start to grow and multiply as the mixture rages through you as it seeks to open you up, making everything seem wonderful once more and reminding you of all the brilliant things that we did together during our golden period. This will then haul you back into the nightmare with me once again.

It is a fact that you will always carry this vulnerability. It is part of our design. It is a necessary consequence of how we affect you. This means that you are always at risk from being influenced from us again and that is why you must remain your vigilance and no contact forever. Do not think after ten years that you can contact me and be safe from my influence. You are always in danger. There is no hope other than to remain away from me because there is always the risk that the mixture will be activated by contact.

If you find yourself in the difficult position of having a permanent connection with us, you cannot implement No Contact. It is impossible. It will not work. Unfortunately for you maintaining no contact is just not a viable option because there is some form of permanent connection between us. Usually it is the fact that we have children together and much as you may like them to have nothing to do with me, you are a decent person and realise that I should have some involvement in their lives. Even if you decide against this I will of course seek redress through the courts. I have not provided in any great detail my behaviour during the judicial process as that is for a different discussion. It will be sufficient to say that engaging me through the court process is not a pleasant experience. Our permanent connection might be because we are neighbours, or that we work together. Alternatively, it may be that I suffer from some illness and if you were to turn your back on me most people would castigate you for doing so (even though it is the correct thing for you to do for the sake of your sanity. Unfortunately, the world still views a physical illness as more real and debilitating than anything mental or psychological. Accordingly, your anxiety, stress and PTSD will fall a distant second to say the fact I am for example suffering from cancer).

The existence of this permanent connection means that you cannot apply the concept of no contact and you are left with trying to minimise contact as best you can. What you must do instead is reduce the potential for me to garner fuel from the interactions we must have. Reduce those interactions to the absolute minimum. When an interaction takes place, if I begin to cause an argument, walk away or end the call. Do not give in to the temptation to 'put me straight' (remember it just will not work with me) or to try and 'make me see sense'. Establish clear boundaries and protocols by which the minimal interaction must take place and stick to them absolutely. Do not deviate.

You can seek to minimise contact in the hope of being able to minimise the impact of your interaction with us. You can seek to diminish the results of our manipulative behaviour by knowing what they are and applying a strategy to coping with them (in that regard I recommend that you read **Escape: How to beat the Narcissist** and **Manipulated**) but you will never ever be able to deploy No Contact. Accordingly, if because of children, the need to care for an infirm relative or the need to look after an incapacitated narcissist, you have a permanent connection with our kind you can never apply the doctrine of No Contact. It is important to realise that, as it is to understand what the doctrine is. Thus, you need to grasp what No Contact is and how it manifests in reality. No Contact is the cessation of all contact and interaction with the narcissist. That is fine as a concept but what does it look like when applied to real life? No Contact operates in two ways. There are those things that we do to establish contact with you (in whatever form) in order to activate the mixture. To implement No Contact, you will need to be aware of what those methods will be, how you can stop them happening in the first place and how being aware of them you avoid succumbing to their allure when they are deployed. The second way in which No Contact operates is in respect of the things that you do that establish contact. Often you might think that it will not establish any form of contact but I will make it clear that certain things that you do amount to a form of contact, which will activate the mixture, and therefore those acts must be avoided and form part of your rigorous application of the concept of No Contact.

Things We Do to Establish Contact

These are many of the steps we will take to try and establish contact with you in order to break No Contact. I have not included the Power Plays as these form a separate and distinct part of the narcissist's response to No Contact and thus merit further discussion below.

- Turning up to meet you at places we know you will be such as home, work, the gym, social environments, shops etc

- Repeated telephone calls

- Incessant text messaging, e-mails, social media messages and the like

- Asking your friends and family about you in the expectation that they will offer up information about what you are doing

- Sending you gifts

- Using our lieutenants to establish contact by proxy by sending them with messages of contrition and asking for an opportunity to talk and discuss matters

- Feigning an emergency in the hope that you will respond

- Broadcasting far and wide on social media how much I miss you

- Using false profiles on social media to get in contact with you

- Using false e-mail addresses or e-mail addresses similar to those of your family, work and friends in order to establish contact

To establish and maintain No Contact you need to be aware of these methods of getting in touch with you and then ensure that none of these methods can be effective. I detail in a later chapter the steps you must take to nullify these various attempts to establish contact with you. Be aware that the use of these methods will be sustained. As soon as you try to establish No Contact you will be subjected to a blitzkrieg effect. I will be explaining more about what happens during this blitzkrieg below so you will be able to prepare for it happening. A lesser narcissist will utilise a number of these methods to try to establish contact. If you are able to resist the contact then the lesser narcissist is likely to move on in a matter of days, as their need for fuel will take them elsewhere. He or she will always be amenable to Hoovering you if given the chance, but if you maintain a heightened defence during the first seven to ten days of no contact a lesser narcissist will move on during this time or shortly thereafter. The greater narcissist will deploy more of these techniques and in particular introduce the Power Plays (see below). The blitzkrieg in the initial stage from the greater narcissist will be intense. Thereafter the effect will lessen but you will feel like you are under siege for some time, as the greater narcissist will not give up on

(a) Wanting to extract the Hoover fuel from you; and

(b) Wanting to punish you.

This means that the attempts to break your No Contact will easily last weeks and more than likely run into months. The greater narcissist will be sustaining him or herself from alternative fuel sources but the desire to break you and bring you back will be strong. By going No Contact, you have criticised the narcissist and the greater narcissist will react considerably to this. His or her fury will be ignited (see

Fury for more on this topic) and the outcome will be a venting of rage in your direction as the greater narcissist hurls everything at you in order to breach your defences. The greater narcissist alongside the Power Plays and the covert methods of establishing contact will use every method of contact above. You are being subjected to a siege and you must maintain your defences at all times in order to prevent a breach.

You may have built your walls up high, closed the gates and reinforced them, lined the walls with archers and ensured several large towers stand in the way of the besieging narcissist. He lines up his siege equipment to try and batter down those walls or burst through the gate in order to establish contact once more and draw on the fuel that you provide. No matter how good your defences it is often the case that the victim him or herself has made a fundamental error and through their own conduct left a rear gate open through which the narcissist can enter and ensnare the victim again. This is where consideration to the second operative part of No Contact must be considered; the things that you do which will constitute contact sufficient for the activation of the mixture and from then on in you are on a slippery slope back to being ensnared by the narcissist again.

Steps You Must Avoid

- Repeated analysis of what went wrong. The message here is simple. You became entangled with a narcissist. There is nothing more to analyse. Accept this was the case. By repeatedly analysing what went on in the devaluation stage of the relationship only means that you are thinking about us and this is a form of contact

- Repeatedly thinking about the golden period. By doing this you are straight away activating the mixture. As I have explained above, the mixture's potency is founded on causing you to experience emotions associated with the golden period. Everything was wonderful then. You experienced some powerful and addictive emotions (all brought about deliberately by us). The awakening of those emotions is what the mixture is founded on. By thinking about the golden period you are establishing a form of contact and activating the mixture. Do not do it.

- Looking at pictures of us. This establishes contact.

- Looking over gifts that we gave you.

- Discussing us with your friends and family. This amounts to a form of contact. Do not instigate such discussions and inform all those who you can rely on that mention of me is henceforth banned in any form whatsoever from discussing what has happened, whether they have seen me walking down the street to even mentioning my name

- Sending a message to find out how we are. This is the empathic individual coming to the fore. You still care. We know this and we count on this as something that will cause you to get in touch. Take it from me that all it takes is one seemingly innocuous message and we will be back in like a shot, charming you and worming our way back into your affections. Don't believe me? Read the Power Plays below.

- Spying on our social media. We are counting on your doing this. You may think there is no harm in having a look at our Facebook profile or establishing a fake profile by which to follow us on Twitter or Instagram. We want you to do this. Our social media will be geared to laying down lots of traps for you to blunder into. We will make mention of how much we miss you, post photos of us together, refer to happy times as well as try and make you jealous by parading a new object of our affections. This will all be done because we completely expect you to be spying on our social media accounts. Once you do you are establishing contact.

- Driving past places where we are just to catch a glimpse of us. We want you to do this. We will be looking out for you doing this. This again is establishing contact even though you may not speak to us.

- Indulging in the Ever Presence that we have established. Ever Presence is one of our most powerful tools. This is a pleasing consequence of all the hard work I invested in the Love Bombing technique. In order to overload your senses and sweep you up in my enticing whirlwind of love and affection I did numerous things to ensnare you. I took you to a park and kissed you beneath a spreading oak tree, pushing you gently against the trunk as I whispered in your ear that this was our tree and we would always come back here and kiss beneath its huge boughs. I ensured that several songs became indelibly imprinted in your mind to remind you of you and me being together. I just didn't go for the romantic ones though. No, I ensured that I selected a range of music to accompany every mood and emotion. That upbeat dance track that is associated with our marvellous holiday in Ibiza. That slow waltzing song that we held each other to and listened to on the balcony of my apartment. That frenetic and energetic rock track that we both jumped around to in your living room. You marvelled at how I managed to select certain songs and pieces of music that you loved and seemed so apt for the moment we were caught up in. You did not know that I had already spent time studying the You Tube videos of songs you adore on your Facebook news feed. I have also wheeled out this play list to several other victims and I know it works. I made sure that you would repeatedly see me sat in the same seat in your kitchen reading a Terry Pratchett book. You would then make dinner as I read aloud to you. We always had a bottle of Rioja on a Wednesday evening. I selected four particular restaurants and took you to them repeatedly. I engaged my lieutenants in reinforcing all the wonderful memories associated with dinner parties, trips to the coast and sporting events. Every day there would be a poem left for you under your pillow. I devoured box sets of Breaking Bad, Poldark and West Wing with you. I even learned pieces of the dialogue, which I would repeat from time to time. I specifically wore the same fragrance, used the same anti-perspirant and shower gel so that this created a particular cocktail of scents, which are forever linked to me. My washing powder and fabric conditioner were chosen to stand out for you. Little do you know I have a notebook, which lists each ex-girlfriend and a corresponding list of smells that I used when I was with you. For you it was Chanel Allure Sport, Dove Men and Care Clean deodorant and Molton Brown Black Peppercorn Body Wash. Not that you have forgotten that have you? The dedication by which I ensured I had imprinted myself on your life in every conceivable sense was worthwhile. Not only did I draw you in and ensnare you, but I also left my mark on you so that once I had discarded you (or if you made the bold move of leaving me) I would forever remain with you. You walk through the park and you are haunted by the image of us up against the oak tree. Somebody gets in the lift next to you wearing Chanel Allure and you want to reach out and hug him as you are immediately taken back to smelling me lying next to you in bed. When *With or Without You* is played you start to sob as you recall how I held you close during a thunderstorm as it played in the background (on repeat of course). Everything I did during the Love Bombing was calculated to trap you but was also laying the ground for infecting the afterwards with me. You see me in books, taste me in certain foods and hear my voice when watching a re-run of a programme. You try to escape by avoiding certain things that are poignant reminders, but that means cutting out certain things that you enjoy. Should you make that sacrifice to someone like me? You are torn. Even if you exercise such discipline, I have planted enough reminders around you that you cannot and will not escape me. You go to the newsagents and see The Times newspaper and instantly remember show I would read it on a Sunday as we lounged after making love through the morning. The powerful memory hurts. I am a spectre that follows you everywhere you go. I know this is happening and it gives me a wonderful sense of omnipotent power. I know that I am in your head and heart on a daily basis. I know how much pain this will be causing you. I also know that I still have several hooks deep inside you and it will not take much if I decided to throw a line to you to draw you back in. You must guard against this Ever Presence. Much of it will creep up on you in the ways that I have explained above and therefore it is hard enough for you to deal with Ever Presence without making it worse by actively embracing it. You may think that because you are not directly engaging with me there is nothing wrong in you listening to 'our songs' one evening as you think back to the happy times you associate with them. You may think there is no harm in your keep smelling that shirt that I left at your house, which smells of my cologne. You are embracing the Ever Presence that I worked hard to establish and by doing this you are establishing contact and triggering the mixture.

- Any form of reminiscence, nostalgia or reflection that involves us, whether you are on your own or with other people. This again establishes contact.

Understand that the siege we will subject you to when we try and break No Contact will be intense, brutal and hard to resist. You need all your strength and awareness to deal with our repeated overtures. You must avoid slipping up and taking any of the steps described above which would in effect allow us to slip back into your mind through the back door, establish contact and trigger the mixture.

No Contact is the complete and total severance of anything and everything to do with us. You must not meet us, speak to us, watch us, ask about us or even think about us. There must be a complete ban on all things to do with us. It is difficult to achieve because your levels of resistance will in all likelihood be low to begin with, you face a determined and committed opponent, you are at risk from making an elementary error on your own part and the pain we have left you in is something you want to get rid of. The easiest and most effective way of banishing that pain is to halt No Contact and engage with us again but in doing this step you are merely subjecting yourself to even more misery and pain down the line.

For No Contact to work you must embrace it in the broadest sense. You must recognise that it means erasing us. You are not allowed the occasional bittersweet smile as you think about a pleasant memory. That is indulgence and a dangerous one at that. You must think and act as if we never existed. Banish us from your existence and never, ever allow us the chance, no matter how small and innocuous it may appear, to establish contact. If you do, the mixture is triggered and you are straight back on the road to engaging with us again.

No Contact means erasing the narcissist from your life in every conceivable format.

No Contact means banishing the narcissist from your life and maintaining that exiled state.

No Contact means that the narcissist never existed.

Grasp this concept and apply it and you will prevent the mixture from being activated with all the dangerous consequences that flow from this. Understanding properly what No Contact actually means is the foundation from which its implementation can then take place. I would suggest that you write out or print out those three comments above and place them on your mirror so every morning you are reminded of the discipline that you must put and keep in place. That is what No Contact is all about.

3 Why is No Contact So Effective?

You will be well acquainted with the repeated recommendation of applying this technique of No Contact. Anybody who seeks to help people deal with a narcissist ultimately advocates the technique. That is because it is very effective. My kind and me despise No Contact for that very reason. Why is that?

All of our manipulation and abuse is geared to control you. It is to ensure that we are the doers and the decision makers. When you decide to go no contact you are wresting that control away from us. That makes us feel small and impotent. It annoys us as it demonstrates that you are not as useless and inferior as we believe you to be. You are flying in the face of what we have always made you out to be. This is a huge act of defiance in our eyes and one that we cannot stand. You are ignoring us.

Our existence is based on two fundamental tenets. Everything is about us and we are in control. No Contact applies a sledgehammer to those concepts and wounds us to the core. Our initial reaction will be one of fury and we will deploy all our tactics to shatter your shield of no contact. We will wheel out every tactic and technique in order to pierce the screen that you have pulled down. Success is paramount. Every day that passes where you maintain no contact sucks away our power and dwindles our potency. Of all the methods available to escape my influence it is the most effective.

. No Contact is regarded as the holy grail of accomplishments when dealing with the narcissist. We hate it. It is designed purely to extinguish our source of fuel and thus it threatens our very existence. Since No Contact amounts to the wooden stake through our dark hearts we will do anything and everything to prevent it, disrupt it and bring it to an end. Moreover, when we are able to Hoover you back in and defeat your attempt at No Contact we feel massively powerful. We have won and you will know by now that we love to win and hate to lose. By having you return to us we are made to feel omnipotent. You may come back broken and dejected, not really wanting to but feeling that you have no choice as a consequence of the manipulation we have exerted over you. Alternatively, you may return under the misguided apprehension that everything is going to be different this time. You may have been conned by us letting you have a glimpse of that heaven again and that blinds you. We may have promised to change, seek help and/or consent to treatment, but it is all an artifice designed to bring you back under our spell.

The damage that No Contact causes to us means we must mobilise every resource available to us to prevent it from succeeding. This is driven by our need for fuel and the promise of the very sweetest of fuels pouring from you when we successfully break your No Contact and have you return to our world. Every single plan, device, machination and scheme will be devised and implemented to ensure the step you will take fails. No Contact is a death sentence to us and must be avoided at all costs. At any cost. You think that you have faced our worst so far? Think again. You will be unleashing the mother of all charm offensives, the granddaddy of manipulations and the thermonuclear setting in our response.

No Contact is so effective because it deprives us of the one thing that we need and that is fuel. We gather fuel in two ways. The first is through positive fuel. This is where praise, attention, admiration, flattery, compliments and so on are sent our way. The manner in which this positive fuel is provided can be through words and/or through actions. It might be somebody telling us that they love us or it might be by someone making dinner for us. This positive fuel is always gathered during the seduction stage. We do not have just one source for this fuel but instead we will harvest it from lots of different sources during a typical day. We select one

31

primary source to provide us with fuel and then have lots of supplementary sources that vary in importance dependent on their relationship with us and also the type of positive fuel they are providing to us. I provide more detail about all of this in the book **Fuel.** With some people we maintain a façade of being a decent person and thus they always respond to us in a positive fashion. This tends to be the case with those who are supplementary sources of fuel. It suits our purposes for a particular friend to think well of us. We do not see this person very often but speak to them on the telephone and we are always content to receive their admiration of our latest achievements, which we will always tell them about. We feel no need to subject this person to devaluation since we do not interact enough with them for their positive fuel to become stale. Furthermore, we regard the maintenance of our external façade as important. This person plays a part in that and we have no desire to alter that state of affairs.

By contrast negative fuel is drawn from such emotional reactions as anger, upset, frustration and sadness. This may be in the form of you shouting at us angrily and insulting us or it might be you slamming a door in frustration. The emotional content of such words and/or actions provides us with fuel. The potency of negative fuel is greater than that of positive fuel. The reason for this is that it is easier to cause someone to be pleasant to us than be nasty or upset. If we achieve an upset reaction it exhibits to a greater degree, the extent of our power over you and thus provides us with a higher grade of fuel. We invariably draw negative fuel from those we are in close proximity to. Accordingly, someone we are in a relationship with will always be subjected to devaluation in order to bring about this negative fuel. You will be familiar with the saying that people always hurt those that are closest to them. This is equally true when applied to our kind. We will always hurt those we are in close proximity to (wives, girlfriends, family members, co-workers) because doing so provides us with excellent negative fuel.

Acquiring this fuel is what we have been created to do. Each and every day we must draw fuel, whether in a positive or negative form or both. It is all that we are concerned about. It fills our thoughts and is the sole driving force behind our existence. We are not interested in loving somebody in order to make him or her feel cared about and loved. We do it so that they respond in a similar way and thus provide us with positive fuel by smiling at us in an affectionate manner or by reason of them taking care of us by undertaking household chores on our behalf. By the same token when we lash out it is because we are driven to do so in order to force an emotional response from you to gather fuel. From the moment we wake until the moment slumber takes us we are driven by the need to gather fuel. It comes from strangers, acquaintances, colleagues, family members, friends and those who we are intimate with. It comes in differing qualities and in varied amounts and each time we receive a dose of fuel it makes us feel powerful and enables our existence to continue.

Fuel is fundamental to our existence. Without it we will cease to exist. This is because we use the fuel to power our brilliance and acquire shards and fragments from others to build a construct of what we regard ourselves to be in order to attract people. We steal elements of other people's personalities, character traits and appearances and create a construct from this. You might it imagine it like a mask or a cloak. Sections, fragments, shards and pieces are accumulated from people we interact with and this fuel allows us to have the power to do this. By creating this mask, we can then attract more people to us who will in turn give us more positive fuel (and in time where appropriate negative fuel). The fuel enables us to create a device to gather more fuel. This fuel is also extremely important for keeping our construct held together and keeping the creature that lurks beneath and who we would much rather not contemplate, imprisoned. This creature reminds us of our failings and weaknesses and it would rather see us cast into the abyss and consigned to oblivion. It is always trying to escape from its constructed

33

prison and the one thing, which keeps it silent and in bondage is fuel. The provision of fuel enables us to maintain the prison construct, which keeps the creature at bay. Should we be deprived of fuel then this construct begins to weaken which gives the creature the opportunity to be heard and make its presence felt. We cannot tolerate such a thing happening, as this will be the start of our downfall. The collapse of our brilliant construct, which bears testament to all of the borrowed traits, which we show to the outside world removes our brilliance. At the same time, the collapse of the construct will allow the lurking creature the opportunity to escape and as a consequence destroy us. We cannot ever allow this to happen. The maintenance of this construct is paramount. The construct both draws in further sources of fuel and imprisons the creature. Accordingly, the maintenance of this construct is absolutely crucial to our continued existence. Maintaining the construct requires fuel and therefore that is why fuel is so important to us, why we need so much of it and why we need it every day.

You are a primary source of fuel. Your continued provision of high-grade fuel be it positive and then negative, is vastly important to us. We need this fuel from you and we need it from you every day. Yes, we will take fuel from other sources because we cannot draw fuel from you continually but you are the most important appliance when it comes to the provision of fuel because you provide us with the greatest quantity and the most potent quality. You may wonder why then is it that we choose to discard you if you are such an important source of fuel? When we first select you, you are shiny and new. You are interesting and alluring to us, as we have carefully selected you to be our new provider of fuel. This excites us and results in our carefully orchestrated seduction of you. We want you. Not because we think you are beautiful, intelligent or talented. We want you because you will provide us with delicious fuel. When we first sink a supply line into you and begin extracting your positive fuel it feels marvellous. It is fresh, invigorating and makes us feel powerful. We cannot get enough of this fuel and this is why during seduction we want to spend so much time with you. We want to bind you to us but moreover we want to keep extracting this fantastic positive fuel from you. Unfortunately, over time you start to fail in your obligation to provide us with positive fuel of a sufficient quality and grade. You do not provide us with the positive fuel to the degree we require and the familiarity by which we know you causes the quality of your fuel to become stale. It is a tale I am used to and I am disappointed each and every time that someone who showed such promise begins to let me down in this way. This results in us needing to acquire a new source of fresh and invigorating positive fuel and accordingly we will hunt down a new victim. We will be preparing them for their forthcoming role as your replacement as we draw them into our world and prepare to extract positive fuel from them. Whilst this is happening we switch to devaluing you because this will generate masses of negative fuel. This negative fuel is even more invigorating and we relish the opportunity to extract it from you. Of course we cannot achieve this negative fuel from you without first having taken positive fuel from you and given you a golden period. If we commenced our relationship with you by devaluing you from the off it would not work. You would not react and most likely you would walk away. We need to give you the golden period during our seduction of you. This creates the positive fuel and provides the contrast so that when we commence our devaluing of you the negative fuel flows freely.

After a period of harvesting negative fuel from you we of course have been cultivating the new source of positive fuel. Thus we are in the happy position of receiving fuel from you (negative) the new prospect (positive) and of course from supplementary sources. Once the new prospect has come to fruition we decide to jettison you. We do this for the following reasons: -

1. The new prospect is providing us with delicious positive fuel. We want to focus our energies on this source;

2. You failed us by failing to maintain the provision of high quality fuel. You must be punished for this; and

3. By discarding you we are setting you up to be Hoovered at a moment of our choosing and the fuel that we extract from a successful Hoover is magnificent. Naturally, we cannot acquire this fuel without first having cast you to one side.

These are the reasons why we suddenly and without warning discard you. We have a new source of fuel in place, we have the supplementary sources of fuel and we have the anticipation of carrying out a Hoover at some point and when we decide to. We are sitting pretty.

Now, having explained all of that to you, you will be in a better position to understand why No Contact is so effective. There are several reasons for this: -

1.   You decide to instigate No Contact, not us. This means you are asserting power and control. Since we regard you as inferior to us, such an act is horrific to us. How dare you actually decide to do something?

2.   You have decided that you no longer want anything to do with us. This is a massive criticism and offends us considerably. We hate to be criticised and by implementing No Contact you are criticising us. You are suggesting that we are not good enough for you, which we regard as a huge blow to our ego. You have always been fortunate to be selected by us. You should be grateful that we chose you and for you now to turn around and tell us that you no longer want anything to do with us is a mortal blow to our sense of greatness.

3.   You are cutting off our supply of fuel from you as the primary source. This means that our construct will start to weaken with the twin consequences that we will not be in a position to attract fuel as effectively as we like and also because the creature may be freed from its prison. We have a complete fear and dread of our construct collapsing and you are bringing this situation about by causing the cessation of our fuel. You are trying to destroy us.

4.   You have chosen the pivotal time to act. You may have done this when we have not secured an alternative source of fuel. By removing your primary supply and doing so when we do not have an alternative properly in place you have caused huge damage to our fuel supply. This creates a huge risk that our construct will topple and causes significant alarm to us.

5.   You have seized control of the situation. We have to control you. We have to control the situation. We have to control the environment around us. We are not used to others exerting control. This sickens and troubles us.

Accordingly, the implementation of No Contact is a highly effective measure because not only are you cutting off the very thing we need, you are creating a huge risk that we may not be able to put in place alternative supplies in sufficient time. You are also landing blows against us by challenging our superiority, attacking our ability to control and mocking our greatness. This is a huge assault on our well-being and in part explains the nature of our response to your implementing No Contact (see below). We must derail it. At any cost. To you.

No Contact can be devastatingly effective because if it is properly prepared for then its execution can be achieved in a moment. This element of swift execution allows you to gain a surprise advantage. It is akin to landing a sucker punch on us and whilst we are reeling from that sudden assault you are able to land further blows against through wrenching away control, demeaning our superiority and challenging our all-powerful status. The effectiveness of No Contact can be distilled down to two main effects: -

1.   It delivers a potentially fatal blow to us;

2.   It has the potential to rid you of us.

I detail below how we react to your implementation of No Contact by explaining why it is hard for you to execute it and also how our immediate response is to cause the supply of fuel to commence again by launching into a Grand Hoover. If our attempts to cause the supply to flow again from you fail, then we are forced to go elsewhere. We have no choice in the matter otherwise our construct will fall and we will cease to exist. It is not the case that we can exist for long without fuel. Yes, we can limp along receiving fuel from supplementary sources but this is not a long-term solution for us. If we chose such a route we would become progressively weaker and weaker. We would find ourselves in a situation of ever diminishing fuel supplies since we would lack the means to gather fresh fuel and the existing sources would become stale, meaning we become weaker and unable to gather fresh fuel. Our power would be diminished meaning we would lack the means by which we could bring about the provision of negative fuel from these supplementary sources. The fuel would become less and less as steadily the construct crumbles and we are consigned to oblivion. By removing yourself as our primary source of fuel we would be left with just supplementary sources of supply. These are not sources that can sustain us. We must fight to resume your supply (and in the same action receive the glorious fuel arising from a successful Hoover) and if this cannot be done we must, we absolutely must, seek a primary source elsewhere. This means that you will be left alone. By maintaining No Contact, the interruption to our fuel supply means we must go elsewhere since you will not longer provide us with any fuel. The removal of fuel in this manner leaves us in an unsustainable position and one whereby we must remedy it promptly. If you will not continue to supply us, then we must find someone else and fast. If you have implemented No Contact when we are in the early stages of the seduction of someone else, you will may witness the frenzied attempt on our part to hurry this new prospect along so they start to gush with positive fuel. We will go into over drive in our efforts to reel in this other person (possibly opting to target two victims such is the urgency of our demand for fuel). These people of this person will be subjected to a thermonuclear love-bombing campaign as we go all out to get the fuel we need. At the same time, we will up our demand on the supplementary sources in order to have them compensate (in the short term at least) for the removal of the primary source. Notably this often means denigrating and devaluing these supplementary sources and you will see us fall out with friends, acquaintances and colleagues as we strive to have negative fuel pumped in our direction. This is a short-term measure. We may be able to extract enough negative fuel from these supplementary sources to sustain us whilst we get a primary source back online, but this cannot go on for long. The reason for this is that the supplementary sources are less bound to us than a primary source. Put simply, a wife is more likely to want to stay and work things out than a colleague. A colleague has less skin in the game and once subjected to devaluation he or she will bail and implement his or her own form of No Contact. It is a calculated risk on our part. Our need for fuel means the concept of friendship, love and camaraderie mean nothing to us. We regard people as expendable in order to achieve our precious fuel. If we must insult our secretary to get fuel and she subsequently resigns, then so be it, we can always hire a new one. What matters to us during this alarming period of the sudden loss of our primary source of fuel are the following:

-

1.   The identification of a fresh primary source immediately;

2.   The binding of that fresh primary source and the provision of positive fuel as quickly as possible;

3.   The utilisation of supplementary sources to compensate for the shortfall. This is a short-term measure and by its very nature will result in the medium term loss of these supplementary sources.

This is a chaotic period for us and our endeavours mean that we have no time to attack you. Should our initial Grand Hoover fail and we realise we cannot recover your primary supply then we kick into this Chaos mode and whilst in it you will be left well alone. This will provide you with a period of respite. This is not a permanent outcome because we will find new primary source and we will replace the supplementary sources we have lost. Once we have stabilised the situation we will be looking to exact our revenge on you for putting us through this hell and also we will still (as we are always) be looking to taste that sweet, sweet fuel from a successful Hoover of you. Thus you may have successfully implemented No Contact and beaten us away but we will always be looking for a chance to breach No Contact. Your vigilance must permanent.

Accordingly, when you implement No Contact the following occurs: -

1. Implementation of No Contact

2. Loss of Primary Source of Fuel

3. Initial Grand Hoover seeking to recover primary source.

4. Hoover is successful - No Contact defeated and primary source is reinstated with bonus of Hoover fuel.

5. Hoover fails - No Contact is maintained. Chaos period ensures.

6. Frenzied attempts by us to identify and implement new primary source whilst draining and losing supplementary sources.

7. Stabilisation. New primary source established. Depleted and lost supplementary sources are replaced.

8. Opportunity sought to effect Hoover against you and defeat No Contact.

By knowing that these stages will occur and also by understanding what is involved in each one you will be better prepared to deal with them and maintain No Contact. No Contact is hugely effective because it threatens our existence and this in turn will ultimately, should No Contact be maintained, cause us to leave you alone and go elsewhere. We will, once stabilised and stronger be sniffing around to try and breach your No Contact and thus the risk will never truly disappear but once you have repelled us through the implementation of No Contact, your aim is to maintain it so we never creep back in. No Contact is the primary weapon you have against us and for the reasons expounded above it is the weapon that causes us the greatest damage and fear.

4. Why is it so Hard to Execute?

Your intended escape and journey into No Contact is one where you will be lined up against the full forces of evil. Make no mistake that we will pull out all the stops in our attempts to derail your escape and claw you back so you fall under our influence once again. You are locking horns with a determined and resourceful foe. We will marshal all our manipulative wiles since our resolve to win this war is huge. You will be run-down, battered, exhausted and drained from our incessant abuse. Your coping mechanisms will be lowered, your self-esteem shattered and your will is about to be severely tested. You should have aimed to muster some of your strength ready for the push to achieve a successful No Contact but chances are we will not have allowed you any respite from the bombarding that we have subjected you to, to allow you to do this.

Our treatment of you may have you wanting to exact revenge upon us. We understand that. You may want to have the last word and fling back in our faces all the hatred, malice and nastiness we have poured over you for however long you have been in our toxic grip. The desire to get one over on us by pointing out what you are doing and why will be overwhelming. You will want to get your side of events in first to all and sundry, telling the world why you decided to escape. You will be itching to tell our family and friends about what we have done and that is why you have decided to depart. This is entirely understandable and we hope that you will engage in these steps. All of them provide us with fuel because you are providing us with attention and emotional reactions. You are also giving us more evidence to show to others about how we are the real victims in all of this.

"Look at how hysterical she is and now she has left without any explanation. How am I supposed to deal with this kind of behaviour?"

"I am seriously concerned about his state of mind. He just flipped out and starting raging at me about all the things I had supposedly done to hurt him. I don't know what to do."

By reacting in this manner you are also stepping on to the battlefield and engaging us on terms that suit us. We are the masters of anger, hatred and fury. Should you embrace those emotions as you try to land one last blow before you commence No Contact, you are doomed to fail. You are signalling to us that your emotional response means you still care about us and thus with this delicious fuel we are encouraged all the more to stop you effecting No Contact. It also tells us that you are not ready and lack the appropriate tools to put No Contact into place in an effective manner. You need cool rational thought. Tempestuous reactions may make you feel better in the short term but they will not serve you well at all.

Put all of thoughts of revenge, clever good byes and final tirades from your mind. They are not what you require here. In preparing for initiating No Contact you must have two aims and two aims only in the forefront of your mind.

1. Protection from potential further abuse; and
2. Diminishing and if possible, extinguishing any and all opportunities for us to get in contact with you.

The first objective is about pooling your resources. If you have to use all your strength to deal with abuse, then you have nothing left to apply to anything else. You need to have the resource available to effect and maintain your No Contact. By removing yourself from the abuse, you immediately free up a source of energy, which can then be better applied to objective two. By focussing on the second objective you are maximising your chances of a successful No Contact campaign.

Liken it to building defences around a castle. If you are too busy using your resources to fight us on the battlefield (where we are at our most potent and effective) not only will you lose that battle and thus lose further resources, you have little or no resources available to build the much needed defences around the castle which will come under attack in due course. Should you switch your resources from the battlefield to the constructing of defences, you can then ensure that those defences are not just a rickety wooden palisade and a shallow trench. Instead you can dig the deep moat and fill it with water, construct high walls, robust towers and line them with troops to repel the invading forces. You can place anti-siege weapons atop the walls and towers. This means that the enemy has no chance of reaching your castle and disturbing you. You are safely ensconced within, untroubled by the carnage taking place outside the curtain wall. You are rested and able to muster a clear mind to direct the continuing defences with a focussed and able approach.

No Contact is hard to execute as a consequence of two things: -

1.   Your empathic traits; and
2.   Our furious determination.

Your Empathic Traits

It is of course your empathic nature and traits, which caused you to be chosen by us in the first place. The fact that you are a caring, honest and decent individual meant that you became a target to someone like me. We know that by exhibiting such empathic traits that you are ideal for our purposes because: -

1.   You are a devotee of the concept of love;

2.   You will readily be swept off your feet by an outpouring of our supposed love for you;

3.   You will respond to our love-bombing of you in a positive way;

4.   You will provide fuel in response to our seduction

5.   You will not depart once our devaluation commences but instead you will remain trying to fix us and heal us. You want to make things right.

6.   You will provide fuel during our devaluation of you; and

7.   You will be susceptible to our attempts to Hoover you.

All of these elements mean that someone who is empathic in nature becomes a prime target for the likes of us. The final reason detailed above as to why you are ideal for our purposes is relevant when it comes to the discussion of why No Contact is hard to execute. The way you are, as a kind person, who cares about other people, who can empathise and place yourself in the shoes of someone else, means that you are burdened with a hindrance from the off when you try to effect No Contact. As you will see with the various Power Plays I will detail below, they play on your nature. You put other people before yourself and accordingly should you see that we are miserable because you have ended our relationship (we are only miserable because our primary source of fuel has been removed - there is nothing else that we miss about you) you at risk of feeling sorry for us. You will immediately be concerned to see that we are unhappy and that we are appearing sad and your empathic traits will cause you to want to help us. You in effect have to fight against yourself in order to maintain No Contact. Every part of your make-up suggests that when you see somebody in need (and let us not forget this is someone who you love and you do because when you instigate No Contact you will still have deep-seated emotions for us) you want to help him or her. If you see upset, you want to bring happiness. Where there is chaos you will bring calm. Where there is fear you will bring hope. This is what you are and we know this. We play on this and the very thing that you are will be the very thing that makes executing No Contact so difficult for you. You find it so hard to walk on by somebody who is hurting. You want to know what has happened to them, how you can help and how you can make things better. When you instigate No Contact with us we will, amongst the various Power Plays and attempts to breach No Contact, present as hurt and wounded. We are appealing to your empathic nature and we know how difficult it is for you to resist this. You will come up with all manner of excuses for justifying breaching No Contact.

"I love him still so how could I stand by and see him so distraught?" (Remember we are only distraught that we have lost our primary source of fuel)

"I am a good person and I could not ignore someone who was hurt." (Only hurt because our primary source of fuel has been interrupted)

"What kind of person am I if I let him suffer?"

"I feel so bad knowing he is alone. He will not be able to cope without me." (We will not be able to cope without your fuel)

You will find all manner of empathic rationales to reach out and breach the No Contact. We rely on this happening.

No Contact is hard for you to execute because you will face pressure from third parties. Some of this will come from our Lieutenants and our Coterie the members of which have been primed to put you under pressure. You will also find pressure being exerted by well meaning others, your friends and your family who actually like us (because of our carefully created façade) and they will be taken in by our tales of woe as we seek sympathy and support from them. They may not be brainwashed in the same way as our Lieutenants but they will rally to support us by suggesting to you that you speak to us and they saw how much "we were hurting without you". In the face of this pressure you will find it very hard to resist reaching out to us and thus No Contact is breached. You will also face the risk of these third parties engineering scenarios so that you and I meet again. They may admit me to their house and invite you around when you are unaware that I will be there. This provides me with an opening to try and win you back from this breach of No Contact. Keep in mind that we have created this façade to everyone else of being a decent person who loves and adores you and this will take him or her in. People also do not like it when a couple splits up. They do not like it for entirely selfish reasons as it forces them to take sides. It is very rare for someone to remain on good terms with both parties following a split. It can happen, but it is rare. Accordingly, when it does happen people are forced to pick a side, even when they like both parties. People find this uncomfortable and resent the fact of being made to choose. Accordingly, people want a couple to reconcile not because they believe it is right for the two people involved but because the preservation of this status quo makes their own lives easier. This translates into you being placed under pressure to make things works with us. You will be badgered and cajoled and you may even find yourself being castigated for being the awkward one (especially since we will have embarked on a smear campaign following your implementation of No Contact) and you find yourself in a strange situation.

You are the victim of sustained abuse, yet you are being made out to be the villain of the piece by not agreeing to reconcile with us. We have kept on good terms with various parties, we have maintained our façade and then sprayed around stories about your own erratic behaviour. I ply the tale that I want to help you and ensure you are stable. Other people see this, they do not want to pick sides, they do not like the idea of conflict and therefore if you do not go along with their wishes to reconcile with us or at least give us an opportunity to discuss matters, you will be seen as the villain. You cannot bear this to be the case and as a consequence you will give in and agree to the suggestions and demands of these third parties. No Contact is breached and once it is you will find it even harder to resist being Hoovered back into our world. We know that our Lieutenants and the third parties will place you under pressure, we rely on it and we know that as an empathic individual you will find it extremely hard to resist.

The very presence of your empathic traits means that you are beginning your No Contact with one hand tied behind your back. It conveys an immediate advantage to us. You would be hard pressed to find anybody who is engaged in some form of competition or conflict who finds themselves so disadvantaged because of who they are. From competing corporations through to combatants in a war through to athletes competing on the track, none of them will countenance putting themselves at a disadvantage through their own make-up, yet that is the very thing that you face because of your empathic traits. You need to understand that your empathic traits are the traitor within and that we will exploit them. You are not a machine and therefore you are unable to switch these traits off and on at will. Instead, you need to realise that these traits put you at a disadvantage, that we rely on this and target these traits and therefore you must be aware of the steps and Power Plays we will apply that seek to exploit these traits of yours. Be aware of how you might react and double

49

your resolve to resist. Gain insight into the ways that we seek to exploit your kindness, your caring nature and your decency and consider ways in which you can counter these attempts. You might wish to explain to third parties in a calm fashion why you are taking this step and if you are able to point to some independent and credible evidence of the abuse you have suffered (something I advocate in **Departure Imminent** as part of your preparatory work for No Contact) this will cause people to understand why you are taking the steps that you are. This will not only validate your actions, it will relieve pressure on you and even may cause those third parties to ally with you against us. Certainly by getting them "onside" in a logical and emotion-free manner (we always hope you will go sobbing and hysterical with tales of our supposed abuse - people are less likely to believe you when you are in such a state) you will lessen the influence we can exert over you through them. This will also remove a "front" from your ongoing battle and give you more resources to confront the onslaught that you will face from us.

If necessary, do not associate with those who are taking our side or those who are pressing you to resolve the matter. They may not react favourably but you need to place yourself first and establish and maintain your No Contact. Eventually our true nature will be revealed to these third parties, especially should you be able to force us into the Chaos Mode (see above) and then you will be able to explain to these third parties why you did as you did and having witnessed our behaviours you will be believed. You will not have the energy or resources to handle intransigent and unhelpful third parties and therefore you will need to jettison on a temporary basis any involvement with them.

Our Furious Determination

As I explained in the chapter above that the act of No Contact threatens our very existence then this means that our reaction to its implementation is one, which is filled with furious determination. I will explain below what happens from the moment you instigate No Contact so you are first hand able to understand what we are thinking and why we respond in the manner that we do. All of this is driven by the furious determination that we exhibit. It is a powerful, scorching and all-encompassing rage, which drives us onwards in our desire to derail No Contact and to preserve ourselves. There will not be any insipid response to your actions. You have mortally offended us and it is this mindset of needing to protect ourselves and punish you for your audacious act of sedition that means we want to breach your No Contact.

We know your weaknesses. This is by design. When we seduced you we ensured that we established all your vulnerabilities. You believed that we were your soul mate, the one, that special person and you gladly poured your heart out to us explaining about the childhood, which was not quite as perfect as you were led to believe, or the phobia you have concerning deep water or the trauma you once suffered at the hands of a family member. Every weakness was explained to us and we misled you as we pretended to care about those foibles and vulnerabilities. You willingly opened your heart to us as you thought that we actually liked you for your candour and these weaknesses. We did not like you for this at all. We did of course like the fact that you so readily told us about these weaknesses. This enabled us to exploit them to maximum effect when we commenced our devaluation of you and now we will do it again. We will seize on your weak points when we seek to derail your No Contact. Nothing is off limits in our attempt to breach your defences. Every vulnerability you have will be used against you, no matter how hurtful because we simply do not care. You have offended us by trying to instigate No Contact and in doing so you have ignited the fury, which churns inside of us. The ignition of this fury is a dangerous matter for you. Whereas in some instances we might use it to protect and shield ourselves as we repaired the damage caused by your criticism of us, in this instance of you implementing No Contact we regard it as an act of war on your part. Our ignited fury will be used as a weapon against you. It will be used to highlight your weaknesses and take advantage of them. Our savage fury of what you have done to us, how could you do such a terrible thing, means that we are imbued with a furious determination which will power the Grand Hoover and enable us to act with a force you have hitherto never witnessed.

This furious determination is akin to waking the beast. You have poked the dangerous foe and now it is our turn to attack you. You have made a huge mistake in taking this step shutting us out and criticising us and accordingly we will respond with every resource at our disposal. We will strive to destroy your defences and pull you back into our influence once again. Our determination is fuelled by desperation to preserve ourselves but moreover by the ignited fury arising from your scandalous act of treason. Even as I write, the mere thought of being treated in this manner by my latest acquisition has me straining with writhing and churning anger. The slightest contemplation of being betrayed by you in such a manner has us on a war footing and ready to attack. We will bombard you, we will assail and assault you as we look to eradicate your defences and bring you back to us. We know we must do this and with such a heightened determination you are in for a vicious and savage battle. You need to be aware of this and you must not underestimate out commitment to achieving our goal. Our very existence depends on it. You must heighten your defences and increase your vigilance because we are coming for you and we do with great fury.

5. What You Must Do

In order to effect a successful implementation of No Contact you must: -

1. Fully understand what No Contact means

2. Be aware of how easily No Contact can be breached

3. Understand the consequences that flow from such a breach

4. Be familiar with how difficult it is to execute and the reasons for this

5. Understand how effective it is against us and why

6. Ensure proper and adequate preparation for the implementation of No Contact

7. Take appropriate steps during No Contact to ensure that it is maintained

I have already addressed points one to five with you above. This chapter concerns itself with the issues of preparatory work and maintenance work on your part. In terms of preparatory work, you must read **Departure Imminent: Preparing for No Contact to Beat the Narcissist** as this will provide you with plenty of detail for the steps you should take in advance of your planned No Contact and to ensure that it is wholly effective. There is more than you might think in the successful implementation of No Contact and by following this guide you will again increase your chances of a successful outcome. Preparation is the key to virtually everything in life and escaping the tendrils of a narcissist is no exception. By reading **Departure Imminent** you will be afforded with all the necessary groundwork and considerations so that when you commence No Contact you will have the best possible footing to then go on and maintain it.

In terms of maintaining No Contact this is when the hard work comes in. You must always keep in mind, as I have discussed above, what No Contact actually means so that you do not fall prey to our overtures or your inherent weaknesses, which may bring about a breach of your defences. You must apply this concept to everything you do once No Contact has been put into place. Everything you do on each and every day must be looked at from the perspective of maintaining No Contact otherwise you will slip up and a breach will occur. Maintaining No Contact is hard work, especially during the Grand Hoover. Should you be able to ride out the initial Grand Hoover then your prospects will increase considerably of maintaining No Contact. When you see out the Grand Hoover you force us into Chaos Mode (as discussed above) and this is when you will be afforded a respite. Use that respite as a time to ensure all defences remain intact and to gather your strength. You will not face a sustained Grand Hoover again you will no doubt be pleased to know. The reason for this is that if the initial Grand Hoover did not work then we go into Chaos Mode and find fuel elsewhere. Once that has been stabilised we have no need of you as our primary source of fuel because we have replaced you. Accordingly, there is no reason for us to expend our energy on implementing a further Grand Hoover. We will of course look to effect standard Hoovers because we want to exact revenge on you for escaping us and also so that we gather some delicious Hoover fuel. This means you can expect further Hoover attempts and thus you must remain vigilant and maintain your defences but it will not be on anywhere near the same scale of the Grand Hoover. Getting through the Grand Hoover will be the hardest part as you are subjected to a sustained campaign that is designed to shatter your defences and Hoover you back in. Maintaining No Contact during this Grand Hoover will be arduous and emotionally taxing but it can be done. To improve your chances there are many things you must have regard to and practical steps, which you can take, which I shall now detail to you.

- Check that there is not a tracking device fitted to your car. A magnet to the underside of your vehicle usually attaches these devices. You would do well to check your car each time before you drive it (if it is left in an accessible place overnight) for any such devices. I usually place them on the exhaust. I do this to enable me to know where you have been and to allow me to just appear so I can see you and try to establish contact with you once again.

- You will have to change your telephone numbers and ensure that I do not get hold of the new ones. You must keep in mind I am likely to have established a Lieutenant or two in your circle (often covertly) so they will leak this information to me. In all likelihood it will take several number changes and the loss of some friends to effect this.

- You should also change your mobile phone itself. There is every likelihood that I will have downloaded software onto your mobile phone that allows me to see your texts etc. from my phone that are received and sent from yours. You need to acquire a clean 'phone. I want this information so I can address any potential threats and also to be aware of your movements so I can "bump" into you and endeavour to Hoover you back into my world. Information is of course power.

- I will repeatedly send you texts and I will use all manner of excuses to try and get you to respond ranging from sending you a message as if it was meant for someone else, feigning an emergency or asking after your children (especially if they are not biologically mine). You will be sorely tested by

56

your empathic traits to respond to these especially one where I make a Pity Play and therefore you need to aim to prevent me being able to send you the messages in the first place. Change your number and take steps to keep its circulation limited to avoid the number being passed to me. As mentioned above it may take several number changes before you are able to remove those people who are leaking me information.

- Bombarding you on social media. The most effective response here is not to be on social media. If you cannot do this, then you will need to block me. I will of course use false accounts to try and follow you or friend you and accordingly you need to be vigilant. I will also have certain of those you engage on social media as my Lieutenants feeding me information. You will find rooting those people out rather difficult. Whilst you will be likely to stop me contacting you, you won't stop the flow of information to me, which I will use to try and contact you in other ways.

- Be aware I will use technology to try and find out about you and contact you. I will search your name in Google to see what can be found there. I may have hacked your Facebook account or you have not been careful enough with your privacy settings, which will allow me to save photos of you for my use and discover details about where you have been and who with. With regard to twitpic and flickr you will have left geotags on your images. I know that most people do not bother to turn off the location metadata that is attached to their photos. I will be able to establish where a photo was taken and see if that is your new home or new workplace. I will be able to ascertain which restaurant you are in having just posted the picture and then turn up. If I know that you have your own domain for business purposes I will conduct a whois search and locate your personal details through that. I will utilise Tineye and Google Images to undertake reverse image searches, which may yield me information.

- I will use other methods of locating you through electoral rolls, city rates property searches and car licence plate searches. I will maintain that I have been in an accident with your vehicle and you then drove away in order to obtain your address details to make a claim from the relevant vehicle licensing authority (and in reality find out where you are)

- Have any computers that I had access to, checked by a professional for software that enables me to access it remotely and read for instance your emails and access banking and other information on your computer. If I know you have financial worries, I will seek to exploit that. If I can see you purchasing certain things and receiving email confirmations this will provide me with ideas for gifts that I can send you.

- I like the fact you upload photos. I will have ensured that when we were together I obtained the exif data from one of the photos that you have uploaded. This data includes the time and date a photo was taken and also a unique serial number. Once I know that number I will be able to locate any photos that you have taken with that camera, anywhere on the Internet. Thus I will soon be able to ascertain which are your photos, when you took them and work out locations and people from their contents, even if you do not appear on the photograph. If you used a smart phone to take the photograph, it gets even better as the GPS coordinates will be included. I do know that match.com and plentyoffish.com do remove the gps information from pictures that you upload but there are many websites that do not.

- When you use a copier all of the information that is copied by that machine is recorded on the hard drive of the copier. It is not going to be difficult for me to organise a copy of that hard drive to look through if I wanted to do this. If we work or worked at the same company, then access is easy and even if we do not I will secure access. I am bound to find some information about you that you have copied at work by running the contents of the hard drive through a scanner searching for certain key words.

- You would be well advised to delete all social media applications as it is highly likely that I am viewing your profiles using fake accounts or that I know your passwords and I am thus able to access your accounts and read messages etc. If you cannot live without them, I would recommend that you delete the relevant social media and set up a new account and be extremely careful whom you interact with, as it may be one of my lieutenants or me in a false guise.

- I will turn up at your house, your workplace, where you shop and where you see friends. I will often just stand and watch so you know that I am there. Over time I will attempt to speak to you and seek to Hoover you back in with false promises of changing and doing things right this time. If you are able to, you must get away from me. Do not answer the door. If I cause trouble in some way by begin abusive or damaging property you need to call the police. Ultimately you may need to obtain an injunction or restraining order to keep me away from your person.

- Be very wary of engaging in online dating. I may appear in another guise. I will also try to recruit someone to date you and then feed back to me about you. I will also use that person to abuse you by proxy. Don't believe me? I have done this to two different people. I knew from hacking into the relevant girlfriends' Facebook accounts that the two men involved were childhood sweethearts and therefore would be willing to reconnect in some way. I ensured they were appraised of how awful you actually were, I advised the men in question that you had said bad things about them behind their backs (it is not difficult to establish some false e-mails between 'you' and 'a friend' talking about how you are just taking them for a ride and not really interested in them) and a financial incentive does no harm either. By deploying this technique, I was able to perpetuate my campaign against two girlfriends who thought they had escaped me. Be aware your former narcissist may well use this tactic. After all, we do tend to think in similar ways don't we?

- I will send gifts to you at home and at work. Do not accept them. Politely decline them and ask for them to be returned by the courier.

- I will send seemingly innocuous items such as paperclips or a piece of ribbon to you. You will know it is from me because I will handwrite your address details so you recognise it has come from me. The intention behind doing this is to send something odd so that you cannot work out why I have sent it and you are moved to get in touch to find out the reason why it has been sent. Remember, we know that you like to obsess over things and you need to know the answers to the posed questions, so we are seeking to exploit this character trait by acting in this manner.

- I will engage in a smear campaign and a character assassination in the hope of provoking you into contacting me to challenge me about what I am saying about you. I will do this myself and do it by proxy too, engaging others to propagate lies about you. I know, because you are a decent person that you will want to challenge what I have said because you cannot bear to have untruths told about you. You need to grow a thick skin. For the most part you can ignore the comments. True friends will know I am telling lies. It will not be pleasant but you need to persevere. If the nature of the allegations becomes serious and repeated you may have to turn to the law to assist, through seeking an injunction or restraining order or even commencing defamation proceedings. Be aware however that by involving the legal process this will bring you into contact with me so you need to think carefully about how you will do this and use a lawyer who is experienced in dealing with people like me.

- I will threaten to hurt myself, lie about having an illness or even threaten suicide if you will not engage with me. Again, because of the caring person you are, I am doing this to appeal to your central beliefs in the hope that you will crumble. You must remain resolute and ignore these protestations. If I do hurt myself, that is my problem and not yours. My kind and me rarely carry out threats of suicide as we actually find doing so contrary to our massive sense of superiority. That is not to say it does not happen, but it is extremely rare. Again, however hard it feels, this was my decision and not yours.

- You must resist any temptation to spy on me. I know how much you want to find out about what I am doing. You know you can look at my Facebook account and there will be no evidence for me to know you have done it, so why not? Every time you look at what I am doing or try and find out through a third party, you are letting me back into your life. This will trigger unpleasant feelings for you and also heightens the risk that your resolve will crumble and you will then fall victim to my attempts to contact you and draw you back in again. I am counting on you lacking the willpower to stay away from checking up on me. That is why I will wait and keep pressing because I know you want to do this. You must never again try and find out about my life in any way. This is often the hardest part because you do not regard it a true contact, but it is a form of contact and one, which pulls you down the path towards being sucked into my toxic world again. It is contact because you are thinking about me and you are going to activate the mixture. Out of the many mistakes that a victim makes when trying to maintain No Contact, this propensity to want to spy on us causes your plans to come unstuck.

- Ditch those friends you know are my Lieutenants and worshippers. You should know by now that they can never be persuaded to think ill of me. You may get along with them still but they will be telling me all about you. They will be mentioning you to me (on my instruction). You may feel you are losing some good things by severing these friendships but they are outweighed by the risks and dangers of maintaining these relationships.

- If you are involved in court proceedings with me be prepared for me to direct all my rage through this. I will repeatedly lie try to con my lawyer, your lawyer and the judge and other officials involved in the case. I will make agreements with you and then break them. I will make you think that a compromise has been reached and then do the opposite. If you are able to avoid having to engage me through the court process so much the better. If you are left with no choice than to do so you must find a lawyer who has dealt with my kind before (otherwise, you run the risk of not being believed and your lawyer being hoodwinked by my behaviour) and you must be prepared for a difficult and long battle. If the argument is about certain financial matters, you may consider that your sanity is worth more than a little extra money each month. Of course if the financial issue is of necessity and/or the proceedings involve children you will have little option other than to engage. In those circumstances ensure that all communication is through the lawyers. Do not be fooled by me appearing and suggesting that we can try and sort things out between ourselves. I have no interest in doing this. I want the friction to continue as I derive fuel from it. Keep a barrier in place through your lawyer.

- Remove trigger items. Again this is hard and some of them may even be expensive and useful but each time you slip on that Tiffany bracelet remember it is my cold, dead hand gripping your wrist ready to haul you back into my personal hell. Delete the photos and the songs, burn the letters and pictures and sell the gifts. Remember the points I made above about handling Everprescence.

- Fill your time. I play on the fact that you will be sat around reminiscing about our good times. You will keep harking back to that because I know that you will not be able to process intellectually at first and then emotionally (for a very long time and probably forever) that you fell in love with the person you thought I was. This despair means you will turn to memories in order to try and manage the pain. This is dangerous. By clinging to the memories you are not allowing yourself to move on from me. By holding onto those memories you are making yourself want the golden period all the more and with that you run the risk of giving up no contact and returning to me. It is very similar to breaking a relationship with an addictive substance. It is so hard to go without the thing you are trying to give up so that you give in and have a drink even though you know what will ultimately happen. I know this and I will prey on this. Accordingly, you need to find new things to do. This will fill your time and lessen the opportunity for wallowing in nostalgia. It will also distract you and give you something else to focus on. Read all about what you have been through. Read more of my books and remind yourself of how hellish it is and how you do not want to return to it. Do not deny what has happened. Yes, it hurts to experience it and you need to embrace the pain or it will build up and become worse. Knowledge really does empower you.

- Join up to forums and communities that deal with what you have experienced. You will make new friends who entirely understand what has happened to you. You will also find that you are helping others (something as an empathetic individual that comes naturally to you) and the pleasure you gain from doing this will assuage the pain you feel.

- You may find that you have little choice but to change your name, use a PO Box and move to another location to escape the ways that I can track you down in order to try and establish contact with you once again and draw you back into my world.

It is very difficult for you to implement No Contact alone. You need support networks. You need these people to assist you in the preparatory stage and even more so during the maintenance of No Contact. Communicating with your support network is a fundamental necessity if you are to be successful in keeping me at bay but the need to communicate also opens up a potential weakness, which I can exploit. The more people you have in your chain of communication the greater the likelihood there is that somebody will leak information to me (either deliberately or inadvertently) and the greater the chance that information about your activities and whereabouts will become available to me. Remember that during the Grand Hoover I will be keeping tabs on all those individuals who I believe can assist me in reaching you. I will be subjecting them to pressure and coercion and the more people you involve the greater the chance there is that one will buckle and provide me with what I want to know.

You need to decide how you will organise your communications once you have embarked on No Contact. There are three fundamental considerations that you need to have regard to when taking this step.

1. Ensuring your preparation does not arouse suspicion or leave a trail which will arouse suspicion as to your activity and aims;
2. How your communications can be achieved effectively with the minimum of fuss and inconvenience once you have departed; and
3. Ensuring that your communications remain undetected by my kind and me, as we will be doing our damnedest to find out how to contact you.

The first and most obvious communication is in person. If you have managed to move away without us knowing where to, then your concerns about face-to-face contact are diminished. If you have achieved a move to a location we do not know about and further the places you will interface with (workplace, schools, shops etc.) are unknown to us then at least initially, any concerns about handling face to face communication with us can be put to one side. Achieving such a position however is extremely unlikely unless you have entered a witness protection scheme or dropped everything and flown to the other side of the world over night without a concern for anything you have left behind and what you will do when you get there.

More likely you will have moved to somewhere we do not know about but you will still work in the same place. Although it may prove difficult in some instances, you can change the places you shop, where you meet friends, the gym or class you attend, the church you worship at and so forth. The workplace can also be changed but this may prove more difficult. Whether there is one place we know where to find you after you have departed or whether there are several places, we will be turning up at all of them, ringing there and speaking to people to find out more about where you are and when you can be found at a particular place. This does present you with a difficulty. If you forewarn all those who you interact with of your intentions, then you are adding more links to the chain and diminishing the prospects of keeping this information secret.

You will need to create barriers and buffer zones where possible. For instance, if you work in an office or in an environment where you cannot be seen from outside we have to penetrate the interior of that building to make contact with you. Do not just leave instructions with those on reception or at the gatehouse or whatever portal exists into the building not to admit Mr A. Narcissist, because we will give false names to those charged as acting as gatekeeper. We will telephone and make appointments under a false name to see you, fabricate an emergency in order to get in contact with you and generate all manner of false pretences so we can get inside to the inner sanctum and see you. I have dressed up as a courier on a couple of occasions with a parcel under my arm in order to breach these outer defences. I have posed as a cleaner in order to access an office block after hours when I knew a former girlfriend would still be working and most likely alone.

In order to try and stop this you should not only provide our names but also a description and hope that those at the entrance remember. If possible, you may be able to send an assistant to greet us and check who we are, collect that parcel or deal with the enquiry so you do not have to risk having to interface with us.

If you work in a place where you are visible from the outside and/or it is easy to access you, then you need to consider having another person with you who can assist in asking us to leave the vicinity and/or record what is happening. If we know who this colleague is we will try and get them on side so that they feed us information about where you are and what you are doing. We will aim to get them to help us out in effecting contact with you and even have them avoid or refuse helping you. Should we keep appearing in this situation you will have to look at ways of absenting yourself and allowing your colleague to cause us to move. Often you will need to use the police to achieve this and seek a restraining order if our conduct is repeated. Again, where possible you should be accompanied by somebody who has not been "got at" by us for the purposes of attending those places which you must attend and that we know you will attend. Be aware of the following: -

1. We know the places that you go to. We have gathered this knowledge through our time with you, questioning of other people and the use of tracking;

2. Once you have departed we will be gathering all the intelligence we can to ascertain which of these places has changed, which remain the same and where the new ones are located; and

3. We will turn up at any and all of these locations on a repeated basis in the
    expectation of seeing you and moreover being able to speak to you.

You will need to minimise the possibility of seeing us and where that is not
possible put in place measures to reduce the amount of time we can remain in your
presence and speak to you. In terms of effecting the maintenance of No Contact,
you must make a list of all the places that you go to. Do not concern yourself with
working out whether we know about them or not, we will know about them. Go
through each day of the week, starting from the moment you wake and jot down
the locations you attend. Once you have done a week, consider any monthly
additions that may occur and add those. With this list you can then decide which
locations can be altered and which cannot. With those that cannot be changed, you
can ascertain how you can put in place safeguards to extinguish or minimise the
risk of us being able to contact you face to face. Be alert to the fact that we will
follow you from a known location, for example your workplace, to learn where you
shop and live, thus you will need to consider alternative routes and checking for
whether you are being followed or not. It will not always be us doing the following
either. We will utilise our Lieutenants and even pay professionals to assist us in
ascertaining your key locations.

Do not use your existing e-mail accounts. Change them to something new.
Maintain a strict guard over who you pass this new information to. You may find it
harder to alter your work e-mail and therefore you will need to guard against e-
mails that arrive from addresses you do not recognise. If possible, forward them to
an assistant to vet with the instruction to send it back if it is legitimate or to delete
it if it is irrelevant. Do not ask them to confirm it has come from us, if they do so,
we have got into your head even if we have not managed to get you to read the e-
mail and this is a breach of No Contact with the risk that the mixture will be
activated. You will also need to exercise caution with existing e-mail addresses. We
will look to highjack the e-mail accounts of others, such as one of your friends

who is a Lieutenant of ours. Furthermore, we will create false e-mail accounts which are very similar to legitimate existing accounts of your friends and contacts in the hope you will not be paying attention and you will end up inadvertently opening it.

With postal communications your best option is to use a PO Box, which will extinguish the prospect of us knowing your new home address. If you remain at an address we know about then still use a PO Box address and if anything is delivered direct to your home, pass it someone else to vet in the same way as the e-mails. If it is legitimate it can be given back, if it is from us or is just junk it can be placed in the bin. Similarly, be wary of postal communications sent to your work address. Have somebody vet those. We will write to your work address and send parcels to them requiring you to sign for them so that we know you have received them. Get someone else to collect them on your behalf and vet them.

In respect of social media, you should shut down all accounts for a period of time until you are very sure the dust has settled and/or you have the increased resilience to swat away a Hoover attempt at a later time. As I have remarked above, most of my kind will engage in a sustained attempt to derail No Contact for a couple of months. If this has not worked, the need for fuel will mean that we cease this campaign and concentrate on others as we are forced into Chaos Mode. We will intermittently try the occasional Hoover however: -

1. It will lack the intensity of the initial campaign and therefore be easier to address;
2. By this stage you should have increased your resilience and strength so that you can deal far more easily with resisting the Hoover.

The malign of us will keep going and thus you will have to maintain the defences, which you have prepared through this preparatory work. With the rest of our kind, having weathered the initial storm you may then resurrect your social media accounts. We will contact you through a Hoover attempt but you will be in a far better position to deal with it. Once you have managed to weather the storm that comes with the Grand Hoover the prospects of some form of contact activating the mixture after this time become diminished. This is because the nature of our attempts to Hoover you will have lessened in intensity but also you will be recovering your coping mechanisms, critical thinking capability and the like as you recover your strength having been removed from our toxic influence. If you do not shut down your social media accounts, you have next to no chance of establishing No Contact for the following reasons: -

1. We will be watching your accounts and you will repeatedly be thinking about this. You need to break this train of thought;
2. You may block us from your various accounts, be we will have our spies who will report back to us what you are posting;
3. The information you post will provide us with intelligence to break your No Contact, for instance showing a new bar you go to; and
4. We will create false accounts and profiles and send you messages and posts. You will be able to block these afterwards but the damage will be done. We will have been able to send a pleading message or a caustic post.

Social media becomes a minefield. You are better closing it all down until a later date. Plus, you will probably find you create time for more meaningful pursuits than garnering likes for your latest cat picture!

In respect of the telephone, you will need to change landline and mobile numbers and remain cautious as to who has this information. Ensure that your phones are set to block all calls, which are withheld. Use voicemail to screen calls if the number is not familiar to you. Make sure your landline displays the number that is calling. If possible, alter your work number. If this is not feasible, then put in place a method of screening those calls through another person. This is easily achieved by altering the programming.

Finally, ensure you change all passwords as we are more than likely aware of them (see **Danger 50 Things You Should Not Do With A Narcissist** for an explanation as to how we get hold of your passwords). We will use this information to ascertain where you are so that we can contact you and we will use the power afforded by this knowledge to wreak havoc against you.

We will use all forms of communication to try and contact you. Therefore you need to either change the way you can be reached and ensure as far as possible that this information does not fall into our hands (because we will be trying to obtain it through a variety of means – following you, speaking to your friends, family and contacts, conducting searches and bribing those who are likely to have the information so that it is disclosed to us) and in instances where you are not able to alter the method of communication you need to consider the ways in which you can put in place screening to create a buffer between us and you.

You must adequately prepare for No Contact and you must then apply the information above whilst you maintain No Contact in order to succeed. The maintenance of No Contact will be the hardest step for you to take as you are subjected to the furious determination we exhibit and you are hindered by the weaknesses, which arise from your empathic traits. Using what I have described so far will give you more than a fighting chance of succeeding. You will need every resource available to you, every opportunity to repel us and all the help you can get because maintaining No Contact is hard. It is at its hardest when you are being subjected to the Grand Hoover, which I will be discussing shortly.

6. How and When Do You Implement No Contact?

You have made the decision that you will implement No Contact. You have undertaken the recommended preparatory work. You are aware of what you must do to maintain No Contact and the next question becomes when should you do it? This is straightforward to answer. You do it on your terms, when you choose and when you feel ready. Do not implement it at the behest of anyone else. In fact, you should not tell anybody when you are about to do it unless absolutely necessary. You should choose when you are going to begin No Contact. By exerting this choice, you will most likely be landing the first blow against us that you have been able to do so in a long time. It will be the first time that you have made a decision, exerted control and done something for you in years. Savour that and the empowerment that arises from it for you will need it to sustain you during the Grand Hoover, which awaits you (see the next chapter). In terms of your timing do not have any regard whatsoever to what we might be doing. Do not think that you should postpone it because we have a busy period at work ahead. Do not delay because one of our relatives is unwell. Do not push back your intended date of commencement for any reason to do with us. You may alter your plans if it suits because of what you need to do but resist at all costs your empathic feelings, which will interfere with your stated plans. You must remain focussed and determined to instigate No Contact when you choose. If you postpone because of us, you are losing control and automatically handing it to us. You will also be losing your resolve to implement it. If you delay for a reason associated with us, you are still allowing us to control you. You are still succumbing to what we want because you have been brainwashed and conditioned to act in this fashion. By thinking about us and how it might impact on us you are allowing us to rent space in your head and this will start to derail the implementation of No Contact.

If you notice that we start making mention of problems that we are having in respect of health, stress, workload, family and such like and we are looking for sympathy you should regard this as an alarm. We may very well have cottoned on to your intentions and we are making Pity Plays designed as a subtle (contrasting with the Power Play approach below) method of getting you to delay and eventually forget about going No Contact. You need to maintain your resolve and ignore these Pity Plays. They are designed to attach to your empathic qualities in the hope that we test your resolve at this early stage and find you wanting.

Remember, the timing of No Contact is entirely down to you. You decide when and once you have done so see it through.

With the question of the timing of No Contact dealt with, what about the method of commencing it? How should this be done?

. The method of commencement is important because if this is not done in the correct way you are doomed before you have even got going. In essence this is about how you let us know that No Contact has been established.

The answer is a simple one. You do not. You give us no indication that you no longer wish to be involved with us. You do not send us a final letter. You do not send a short explanatory text. You do not call us to explain no matter how much (as a typical empathic individual) you feel the need to do so. Do not fall into the trap of thinking that you owe us an explanation. Have we ever explained ourselves to you? No. Why then should you? Oh I know the empathic traits you have are crying out for you to explain politely and in a civil manner why you are taking this step. Part of you may even think that you should have one last pay-off by bidding us good-bye in order to make you feel better. Why shouldn't you engage in giving us the kiss off after everything we have done to you? Surely it will feel empowering, liberating and a sense of triumph to tell us where to go? Yes, it might but it will also open you up to allowing us to immediately try and halt No Contact before it has got going by launching one of the Power Plays at you. You may feel determined but I know from experience that if you give me the chance to launch a Power Play at the outset of No Contact I stand a very good chance of winning you back. You may not believe that but accept this fact from as seasoned practitioner. In all the instances where a former girlfriend of mine has decided to apply No Contact but has wanted to do so in circumstances where she gets to sign off with some kind of valedictory speech, she left the door wide open to me launching a Power Play and they all succeeded in winning them back. All of them. By way of example, let me recount the circumstances to you of when Kathryn attempted to leave me and instigate No Contact. Kathryn was a former girlfriend of mine who followed on from Paula. It was October and the leaves on the trees had just begun to turn. It was a Tuesday afternoon and pale, watery autumnal sunshine spilled into the living room as the day meandered towards its conclusion. Twilight had not yet commenced and the clocks had yet to be put back, so when I returned from the office it remained light. Kathryn was sat on the edge of the sofa with a suitcase next to her. We had lived together for around six months at this point. I walked in contemplating the social media flirtation that I would engage in later that evening and saw her sat there, staring ahead.

"Going somewhere?" I remarked.

"Yes. I am leaving."

"Leaving?"

"Yes, I am leaving you. I have had enough of you. I don't fully know what has happened because everything started so brilliantly but lately, well, you have become something else and I don't like it. You are nasty and cruel to me and it is clear there is something wrong with you. I have to leave and that is all there is to it. I am going to go and you must not contact me, do you understand?"

"No, I don't understand," I responded as I felt the emptiness rising up to try and claim me. She stopped looking ahead and turned to look at me. I could see the nervousness in her eyes.

"Look, I have been doing some reading and there is something the matter with you, HG," she began.

"Something the matter with me?" I questioned. She nodded slowly.

"Something the matter with me?!" I exploded as my voice rose. She jumped at the sudden escalation in volume.

"You sit there, in my home after I let you live here, after all the things I have done for you and you tell me there is something wrong with me? How heartless can you be? I have been working my balls off for the last month to ensure we can go away next month on a cruise. It was meant to be a surprise but I may as well tell you about it now seeing as there will be no point in going."

"A cruise?" she said weakly.

"Yes, I thought we could get some winter sunshine, you know, to cheer you up as you told me that you find winter hard, so I have been working like a Trojan to get this deal done so I can get away and take you away. I may have been a bit short with you at times but that's only because I have been tired and the deal has been preying on my mind. It is a big one, the biggest in the firm's history and they decided I should lead it. Do you realise how much responsibility that involves? I am there slaving my guts out and you are saying there is something wrong with me. I cannot believe it. Actually, yes you are right, there is something wrong with me, I am too damn kind to you."

My tirade continued as I dredged up from my memory all the wonderful and kind things I had done for Kathryn during my seduction of her. The fact there was no cruise was an irrelevance. How dare she decide to leave me and how dare she suggest that I had something wrong with me. I kept up the anger as I marched back and forth, arms waving, leaning in to vent my spleen in her face as she sat in stunned silence. On and on I went, recounting my generosity and largesse before railing against the cruelty and injustice of her treatment of me. Eventually the sobbing began, but I did not let up in the intensity of my berating of her. After perhaps an hour of this I eventually sat next to her and lowering my voice said,

"I know I don't always get things right but I am doing my best for us. Please understand that."

Wiping away the tears she turned and gave me a slight smile.

"I know, I am sorry, I guess I just got lost in thinking about myself and didn't realise what was behind it all. I know you work hard and have a stressful job, I just felt that I was no longer valued by you."

"You are always of use, I mean value to me, you know that," I said as I slid my arm about her.

"Thank you."

"Now, let's put this case away shall we and go out for dinner, you can choose."

She nodded and thanked me again. She was going nowhere. Kathryn had made the fatal mistake of giving me an opportunity to engage her and in doing so I was able to launch a Power Play and defeat her attempt before she even got out of the door.

Accordingly, your narcissist may not have the charm and skill set that I have but even so why take the risk of failing before you got going? No speeches, no send-offs, and no theatrical announcement whether in person, text, message, telephone call or banner dragged behind an aeroplane. Do not hand us the advantage by announcing what you are doing.

In order to reinforce this message, let me provide you with another example of a former girlfriend who thought she could depart and instigate No Contact. Like Kathryn, she made the mistake of speaking to me and telling me of her intentions, which gave me a sufficient opening to frustrate and deny her intentions. This girlfriend was Lesley. You may remember that I liked to refer to her as "It" in order to provoke a reaction from her. I had been involved in a badminton competition and I comprehensively demolished my opponents resulting in me returning home earlier than expected. I walked in to our house to find Lesley walking towards me carrying a box. I noticed that there were at least half a dozen other boxes placed in the hallway. She halted as I walked in and just stared at me.

"What's going on?" I asked.

"Er, I," she mumbled. I moved over to one of the boxes and opened it. Inside I could see various books, all of which belonged to Lesley. I opened the next box and inside there were ornaments and similar paraphernalia.

"Having a clear out are we?" I sneered sarcastically.

She set the box down and drew herself up to her full height. The effect was more comical than authoritative.

"In a way yes, I am clearing out of your life. I have finally worked out what you are and it makes sense, especially after the way you have treated me the last month. Sandra has helped me recognise what I have been living with. I did not see it and I feel stupid but now I know and I know that I have to get out and stay out."

"Sandra eh?" I remarked as I stood blocking the doorway.

"Yes, she has been telling me that you suffer from a personality disorder, you are a narcissist. Apparently you cannot help it but you are only ever going to treat me badly for your own purposes and I am not going to be subjected to that anymore."

"My own purposes? It is interesting that you say that. I think you will find that somebody else is using you for their purposes and it is not me."

"What do you mean by that?" asked Lesley confused.

"Do you not think it strange that it is Sandra who is feeding this ridiculous idea of you leaving, to you?"

"No, I mean, she is my friend, she has my best interests at heart, unlike you."

"Really?"

"Yes," she answered but I could see the uncertainty across her face.

"Sandra is a liar. She lies to you on a daily basis although I must admit that I am somewhat taken aback at her suggesting I have some kind of personality disorder, that is a new low Mind you, from what I understand of such conditions, the sufferer tends to suggest that others are suffering from it and not them. It strikes me that this is an archetypal response from Sandra. She is putting her problem onto me. Well actually us."

"What are you talking about? She showed me the articles and it make sense when I compared your behaviour to what is in those articles," replied Lesley.

"She is manipulating you. You have not been yourself as of late. I have been concerned about you actually, you seem tired all the time and, please don't take this the wrong way, but it makes you tetchy and irritable. You have been snapping at me a lot."

"I haven't, well, I mean, I know I have shouted at you, but that is because of what you have been doing," she answered but the conviction drained from the sentence as she spoke it. I raised an eyebrow as she stopped speaking. "Come on, it is alright. I did not want to say anything to you for fear of upsetting you. I know you have had a lot on your plate as of late."

"What do you mean? I am confused. What have you not wanted to say anything about?"

I gave an exaggerated sigh.

"Sandra has been flirting with me. She is trying to break us up."

"What?"

"Yes. She wants me for herself. I told her that I would not leave you but she is determined. That is why she has been whispering in your ear in order to make you believe her lies and leave me."

"I don't believe you," responded Lesley but I could tell she was unsure. I reached into my pocket and extracted my mobile 'phone. As she stood mouth ajar and eyes wide in astonishment I found the messages that Sandra and I had been exchanging. I had instigated the contact and she had responded to it, sending a succession of messages, which made her desire for me evident and her intent clear. Her messages had arrived when I was busy talking to someone else in a bar, so there was a stream of nearly a score of these fruity communications with no response from me. I scrolled to them and thrust the 'phone under the nose of Lesley. She read the message and I moved onto the next and then the next and then the next. Her eyes began to well up with tears and then she shoved my hand away.

"There are more, I am afraid, as you can see, I hadn't responded, but she kept sending them," I explained as I moved alongside her.

"How could she do something so low, she said you were the problem."

"Jealousy makes people behave in strange ways," I suggested "and it is clear that she has some kind of mental disorder, you would have to, to behave in this manner."

"The bitch, I am going to call her and tell her what I think," said Lesley her anger flaring up.

"Leave it, she will only deny it won't she, but I have shown you the truth. Listen, someone like her wants you to react, she gets off on it, that is how sick she is."

"But she deserves to know I have found her out," protested Lesley.

"I can understand that, but she will enjoy seeing you angry and upset. Knowing how twisted she is she will probably be encouraged to keep trying. No the best thing that you can do is just ignore her. That will really get to her. Don't speak to her ever again. She has destroyed your trust and your relationship. Forget about her."

Lesley considered this for a moment, the tears still flowing.

"You are right, as usual. How could I have been so stupid to fall for that?"

"Don't beat yourself up about it my love, people like her are skilled at manipulating people. It is not your fault, this is what they do and you never see it coming. You need to focus on you and me and not bother with her again. That will stick two fingers up at her and it will driver her crazy trying to work out why."

Lesley nodded.

"Come on, I will give you a hand unpacking these boxes," I smiled and squeezed her shoulder.

"Thank you. I am so sorry to have doubted you, I feel terrible."

"It happens. You have made a mistake," I added as her upset fuelled me. She leant in to me and wrapped her arms around me as I looked up and smiled at my reflection in the hall mirror. Once again an opening had been provided to me and I took it.

What do these two women have in common? They failed to prepare a game plan for establishing No Contact and thus they failed miserably. There are other examples where I have derailed No Contact before it has begun or during its existence and these are detailed in the Power Play chapter below.

If you do not prepare and have a game plan, you will fail before you even begin. Just like Kathryn and Lesley.

Remember those silent treatments you were subjected to? Of course you do. You will recall how they came out of nowhere, how they lasted for hours or days or maybe even weeks but most of all you will recall how devastating their effect on you was. Now it is time for revenge. When you decide to implement No Contact you are in effect giving the narcissist the silent treatment. Just go straight to No Contact. No announcement, no explanation and no foreshadowing. Instigate it when you decide and immediately you have seized the advantage. You have decided when it is to be implemented. You have implemented it without any initial response from us (which is the most dangerous time and the time when you are susceptible to being sucked back in). You have avoided giving us a platform from which we can launch a Power Play and you can have the satisfaction of using one of our most powerful manipulative tools against us. You decide when to start No Contact and just do it.

You will have an overwhelming desire to try and take revenge against us for the way we have treated you. Do not bother. You will want to signal to the world that you are free of us. Resist that temptation as you may slip up and provide some useful information to us (remember, the more people you involve as links in the chain, the greater the risk you run of not succeeding) and also the fact you are telling everyone provides us with fuel. It also means that we will want to complain about your conduct in order to garner sympathy. You will also feel the need to provide a final sign-off to us. Doing it in person is idiotic; your campaign of No Contact has failed as soon as you start talking to us. You may like to write a letter or leave a video outlining all the reasons why you have gone. Tempting as this may be, do not do it. You might think it affords you some kind of closure (believe me you are light years away from obtaining closure from us since even if you manage

No Contact we will keep appearing in your head and in your heart) or that it is cathartic in nature. All you are doing is giving us more fuel by providing us with attention and also igniting our anger. We will not pay any attention to the content of what you have written. We will not sit and think,

"Oh yes, I had not looked at it like that, she has a point. What a terrible person I am."

We will not reflect or feel shame, guilt at hurt at however brilliantly composed your final riposte to us is. We will feel anger. Anger that you are making us feel small. Fury at the audacity you have exhibited in escaping us. Rage at you seeking to diminish our natural superiority. The consequence of this is that your aim has not been achieved and you are giving us even greater motivation to find you, punish you and return you to our nightmare world.

If you really must convey to us in some way that the relationship has ended, although I recommend you just commence your No Contact, if you feel you must send some kind of message then you organise for a third party to deliver a note to us that is straight to the point.

"Dear

I have ended our relationship. I do not want to see you or have any contact with you.

No longer yours............."

That will do the job and avoids generating fuel for us.

Accordingly, you should not concern yourself with: -

1. Having the last word;
2. Telling us what we are;
3. Proving you are right;
4. Discussing financial and legal ramifications of the split;
5. Making arrangements to return any possessions of ours (that can be facilitated later through a third party);
6. Telling others about what has happened.

Forget about our immediate reaction and us. You need to maintain the preparations you have put in place and focus on now maintaining the No Contact that you have established.

7. The Grand Hoover

Accordingly, No Contact has commenced. You have not trumpeted its arrival nor crowed about deploying it against me. Instead you have lowered the portcullis, closed the shutters and pulled up the drawbridge as you sit ready and vigilant. The siege is coming. The siege where the affronted and enraged narcissist assembles all his manipulative tools devised to establish contact once again so that you return to him and thus he can drink deep of your potent fuel. It is fundamental for you to understand what you can expect to happen from the moment we become aware that you have instigated No Contact because from that instant we will commence a Grand Hoover as we seek to suck you back in to our influence. I will now take you through what will happen.

We will apply repeated Hoovers against you during the period of No Contact but we will always start out with a Grand Hoover which is designed as a very powerful opening salvo on our part designed to shock and awe you into submission in a devastating assault against you. This is in effect the unleashing of our blitzkrieg.

Blitzkrieg is a German word meaning "lightning war". It is used to describe a method of engaging in warfare where the attacking force engages in short, fast and powerful attacks with the intention of breaking through the opponent's defences. The attacker will then dislocate the defenders by the use of speed and surprise. A blitzkrieg attempts to unbalance the enemy by making it difficult for them to respond to the repeatedly changing front with a view to ultimately defeating them in a decisive battle of annihilation. When we learn that it is your intention to leave us as part of a campaign of No Contact or to commence No Contact we unleash our own blitzkrieg in order to stop it before it is even started. How is this blitzkrieg effected? Just like the German blitzkrieg, which uses a variety of mechanised methods of combat combined with air support, we use an array of techniques against you.

1. Fury. Not only are we mortally offended that you could ever think about the cessation of our relationship and begin to take steps to achieve that, we know that a burst of anger is a very effective way of bringing you back under our control. The use of fury is twofold: -
   a. It is an immediate response to flood us with power to eradicate any feeling of weakness that arises from you challenging our superiority through your attempt to leave us; and
   b. It is used to stun you. The ferocity of our rage is designed to have you immobilised for fear of what might come next. You do not reply, you do not move, you remain rooted to the spot and thus this enables us to roll out the other constituent parts of our blitzkrieg.

2. Pleading. We will beg you to not end the relationship. We will beseech you, cajole you, issue earnest promises to change and seek help, we will vow to improve and help you more, we will allude to bringing back the golden period (we cannot actually bring it back in the instant of the blitzkrieg as time is against us) and even turn on the water works. This appeals directly to your sense of caring and your innate belief that there is good in everybody. You will also be so relieved that the fury has ended. We know this. Having subjected you to the rage, we now offer you an escape route from it. We make you feel like you have the upper hand as it is your decision to now let us have another chance. The reality is, we have made it the lesser of two evils. You cannot stand to be on the receiving end of our anger, you do not want it to return and therefore in all likelihood you will cave in to our pleading. We know this. This is why we do it.

3. We will hang around you so that you are not able to concentrate on progressing your now discovered plans. By occupying your time (much like

an invader occupying a country) we will cause you to be bogged down in dealing with us and not able to move forward. We will combine this occupation of your time with our pleading.

4. Whilst we keep you occupied we will be using our Lieutenants to spread the word that you were going to end the relationship after everything that we he had done for you and in such a hurtful way by acting in a pre-meditated fashion. The aim of this is to turn opinion against you, have people support me (and not you) and again add another obstacle for you to overcome should you try and persist in escaping us.

All of this makes it harder for you to get away from us and thus means that your prospects of effecting No Contact are much diminished. Indeed, from experience I can tell you that our use of the blitzkrieg is highly effective and in most cases results in your backing down, giving us a further chance and becoming subjected to our behaviours once again. Of course, once we know you have changed your mind, we will then have the time to give you a delicious dose of the golden period for a while. This reward will convince you that you have made the right decision. It also lays down a precedent. Should you try and escape again in the future, we will blitzkrieg you and we will remind you that everything can and was all right again (we will naturally gloss over the eventual return to the abusive behaviour again) and you will feel that warm, glow as you recall being allowed to enjoy the golden period again. The blitzkrieg is very effective. You do not want to be subjected to it, as it will most likely halt your plans before they start. You must not give us an opportunity to deploy this technique against you and therefore you must ensure that we are given no prior notice of your stated intentions. Any loose lips will result in us learning about what you are planning and our response will be swift, brutal and effective. We do not want to lose face by having someone we regard as inferior outflank us. We not want to have to expend energy in replacing you as a consequence of your decision (we decide when we want to get fuel from a different source, not you) and we do not want to lose a source of fuel that is serving us so well, that we have invested time and energy in and one which will continue to provide this fuel for some time to come. Our blitzkrieg is solely designed to enable us to hang on to what we have already got and it will torpedo your plans if you allow us to unleash it against you.

It is worth pointing out at this juncture that the intensity of our Grand Hoover will be governed by several factors: -

1. The readiness of our alternative primary source to provide us with the required level of fuel;

2. The levels at which supplementary sources are supplying fuel;

3. The nature of the narcissist you are dealing with (lesser of greater)

This access and your timing of the implementation of No Contact will have a considerable impact on how intense and for how long the Grand Hoover will last. If you have chosen to implement No Contact when we have only just begun organising an alternative primary supply (and furthermore if our supplementary sources happen to be functioning below optimum) and you are involved with a greater narcissist, then you can expect an intense and frenzied Grand Hoover. This is because our alternative sources to provide us with fuel are not functioning at the required level. Thus we need to Hoover you back and quick. We will launch our blitzkrieg and sustain it as we engage in total war against you, as we need you back supplying us.

By contrast, if the Grand Hoover does not last long and lacks intensity it is likely that you have been locked with a lesser narcissist who has the alternative source up and running already (and thus you were close to being discarded anyway) and also the supplementary sources are functioning well. Since every we do is governed by our need for fuel, if we have fuel to hand then the Grand Hoover will be lessened in terms of intensity and duration. Accordingly, if you implement No Contact and your narcissist barely seems to react you can be safe in the knowledge that you were on the cusp of the discard and he is able to turn to his alternative fuel easily. There will still be a Grand Hoover. Do not think it will not happen although it will be on a much-reduced scale. It will still happen for two reasons: -

1. The prospect of harvesting Hoover fuel from you; and

2. The ignition of his fury arising from YOU making the decision to end the relationship and not him.

It will however not last for long as if it becomes quickly apparent that you are maintaining your defences a narcissist in this position will give up the ghost and attend to those sources, which are yielding fuel easily. He will not want to waste energy on you for long. Do keep in mind however that there will be future standard Hoovers. The opportunity to acquire some Hoover fuel from you remains too tempting.

Accordingly, the response of your particular narcissist will be governed by the factors described above and these will impact on the duration and intensity of the Grand Hoover. Beware if you are involved with a greater narcissist who has only just begun arranging an alternative primary source and who has less than effective supplementary sources. You are in for a bumpy ride.

When we first work out that you have decided to get rid of us and therefore you have implemented No Contact the first thing that will happen is that our fury will be ignited. You have criticised us by choosing not to be with us any more. We do not regard this as a choice you are allowed to make. We do not recognise the legitimacy of your decision and therefore this will amount to a massive criticism of us. We hate criticism as it drives a dangerous blow against us. In order to protect ourselves the churning fury that exists at all times within us becomes ignited and this will then be used as weapon against you. Enraged we will go on the attack using the power surge from this ignition of our fury to power our actions against you.

Our sole aim now is to make contact with you for the purposes of effecting the Grand Hoover. We need to find you and then contact you. Nothing else matters. Our first step will be to make contact with you. We will telephone your mobile, work phone and home landline in order to speak to you. We will send text messages, social media messages and e-mails in order to bring about a response from you. The content of these messages will accord with some form of Power Play, which I detail in the next chapter. We will leave messages with your friends, family and colleagues as we try and find out where you are. We will attend on your home, your work and then your family's residence and the homes of your friends in order to try and find you. Our energies will all be channelled into locating you and you can already see from the wide range of places and methods by which we will try and get into contact with you, you have your work cut out in either ensuring those methods of communication will not work (changing mobile telephone number, shutting down social media accounts etc) or that the prospects of them working are minimised (effecting a gatekeeper at your place of work if you have had to stay at the same place). We will be trying all conceivable methods that will allow us direct contact. We will not care for boundaries as our furious determination and our desperation to have you reinstated, as our primary source of fuel will be driving us on in this exercise. Every piece of information will be used to try and find you. If we manage to locate you, we will attend in person because we will want to speak to you. We will try and gain admittance by whatever means we can to the place where you are. This underlines the importance of you placing yourself in a location that we will not know about during the Grand Hoover. If we find out where you are we will try and see you. We will turn up at whatever place it is and demand to see you, we will harass other people in order to force them to see us. You will feel under considerable pressure, especially if other people are being sucked into this situation, to speak to us in order to try and calm us down. We are counting on this being the case. We will ask people to pass messages on to you and unless you have effectively briefed these people not to do so, they will act on our request. This happens because they do not understand whom they are dealing with and how fundamental it is for No Contact to be maintained. Other people, especially those who do not know me will think that it is just the usual up and down nature of a relationship and there is no harm in admitting me to see you or at least passing a message on. Again we count on knowing human nature for this to happen. We know that if we can get a message to you encompassing our Power Play your resolve will weaken and there is a good chance that you will then grant us an audience. This will then result in the Power Play being extended or another one being used as we Hoover you hard. Our aims, once we realise that you have ended the relationship and you have instigated No Contact are as follows: -

1. Locating you;
2. Conveying a message to you;
3. Seeing you face to face

We will keep trying to establish these three aims. We will muster every resource available to us, utilise every manipulative technique to get people to assist us and give up information about you or convey information to you. We will pull no punches in our attempts to garner pity and sympathy for our distressed sense. It is all a ruse.

If in these early stages, we are struggling to establish any of these aims we will commence a character assassination and smear campaign against you. The purpose of this is to generate more sympathy for our situation and make you appear like the villain. This is designed to get one of the links in your chain to snap and provide us with your location, convey a message and/or facilitate a face-to-face meeting with us. Nothing is off limits in terms of the things that we will say about you. We want people thinking you have committed a grave wrong against us. We want people to be sympathetic to our situation and we also want to show them that despite what you have done to us we want to resolve matters between us. How noble are we? This is bound to cause someone to blow your cover and point us in the right direction.

If we cannot get to you from the off, we will focus our attention on all known links that you have. Family, friends, ex-boyfriends, colleagues, associates, acquaintances and so on as we will press them to reveal where you are. We will pressure them to confirm they know where you are even though they may not reveal the location to us. In such a situation we will then coerce them to convey a message to you in the hope that from this chink in No Contact we can then drive a bus straight through it and destroy your No Contact.

This initial Grand Hoover will last between one and four weeks, which is dependent on the nature of the narcissist you have been involved with. If your narcissist is of a lesser nature, then the Grand Hoover will be a few days before he gives up and turns to replacing you with a new primary source. The more malign and greater narcissists will apply pressure for longer and will do so for weeks in order to get to you. Eventually they will have no option, because the Chaos Mode has engaged, to seek a replacement and draw on the supplementary supplies.

This Grand Hoover is never just one telephone call or one text message or one attempt of knocking on your door. Those are standard Hoovers and they may come later during the stabilised period. During the Grand Hoover the attempts to locate you will be determined and focussed. Once we have located you then the attempts to contact you will be made frequently and in a wide variety of methods. The Power Plays will be unleashed and usually more than one. You will feel under siege and therefore if you have been able to achieve a situation of removing yourself to a place where we do not know where you are you will be in a very strong position to ride out the initial storm. If we cannot locate you then this forces us into the Chaos Mode quicker. We realise that fuel is being drained and that there is no immediate prospect of recovering it from you, as we do not even know where you are. Accordingly, the Chaos Mode will kick in at an earlier stage and we will seek our alternatives and give up (at least for now) trying to find you.

If we know where you are this provides us with encouragement and therefore the arrival of the Chaos Mode will be delayed as we are spurred on by the prospect of being able to engage with you. If we are able to see you even if we cannot engage with you then this will provide us with encouragement as well. Accordingly, if you find yourself in a position where you can manage to avoid engaging with us but you cannot stop us watching you, be prepared for the Grand Hoover to continue for longer. Seeing you will give us hope that we will be able to engage with you and thus we will keep at the Grand Hoover for longer.

What you must keep in your mind is that the Grand Hoover cannot go on forever. The intensity of this Hoover and the varied means by which we try and effect it will have you reeling but it will only go on for so long until our fuel level has diminished and the Chaos Mode kicks in. At that point we have no choice but to seek out a new primary source of fuel and for us to call heavily on the supplementary sources. When this happens you will see a cessation in our attempts to find you or engage with you. At this point you can pat yourself on the back because you have weather the Grand Hoover. You have seen off the first and most powerful attempt to bring you back into the fold. You have maintained No Contact for a suitable period, which has resulted in the diminution of our fuel supply so that we have been forced into alternative action and thus have broken off our Grand Hoover attempt against you. You have won the battle and a major one at that, but of course the war will rage on and we will be back, albeit on a lesser scale at some future point.

Maintaining No Contact during the Grand Hoover is the hardest thing you will do. Everything is designed to breach No Contact. From your own vulnerabilities, to the risk of third parties allowing contact and our own furious determination to break No Contact. Central to the Grand Hoover are the application of the Power Plays which is what we turn our attention to next.

8. The Power Plays

The Power Plays are part of the Grand Hoover. These are classed into particular categories and are designed to Hoover you back into our world. You need to know what these Power Plays look like so that you can be alert to them and increase your resistance. If you do not know what they look like you are more susceptible to being Hoovered. The reason the Power Play is so effective is because firstly it has already breached No Contact by virtue of the fact that you are considering it. Secondly, the design of the Power Play is such that it plays to your empathic instincts and therefore proves hard for you to resist. The Power Plays can be conveyed to you in many different forms. It may be in a telephone call or message, a text message, a note, a message conveyed through a third party or an e-mail. For maximum effectiveness we prefer to be talking to you face to face when we unleash a Power Play against you. If we are able to do this, we stand a very good chance of overcoming your resistance and therefore Hoovering you back in. It stands to reason therefore that if you manage to implement No Contact and do so from a place where we do not know where you are and therefore we have no method of establishing contact then the Power Play cannot work because we cannot expose you to it. If you manage to place yourself in an unknown location and nobody else conveys that location to us, then the only person who can defeat No Contact is you. We cannot find you and therefore we cannot contact you and we cannot use a Power Play. This underlines the massive advantage that is conveyed to you if you are able to remove yourself to a place we do not and cannot ever know about. Of course, life is never so straightforward as to allow this to happen simply, but if you can achieve such a position then that is what you should aim for.

In the majority of cases however you will not have been able to transplant yourself (for reasons of family, friends, work, money or convenience) to another location and consequently this increases the risk that we can establish contact with you and in turn we can unleash a Power Play against you. In those circumstances you need to know what these Power Plays look like so you know exactly what they are. They are an artifice designed to Hoover you back in. There is nothing true or legitimate about them and you must understand and reinforce that message to yourself. Accordingly, I will now turn to the various and most common Power Plays that we will apply against you. There are others but I have selected the ones used the most for the purposes of universal applicability. By now you will be familiar with the fact that our kind operates in very similar ways and therefore you can expect to be subjected to one or more of the following power plays when we try to break your No Contact.

8.1 Emergency!

We will start with the Emergency Power Play because this is one of our most popular methods of establishing contact and Hoovering you back into our grip. It is popular because it is most effective. It is an excellent Power Play because it will serve as a method of establishing contact and then we are able to expand on the nature of the emergency once we are with you to allow us to apply our manipulative manner to good use against you. If we still able to effect some form of contact with you, we will most likely send you a text message with the intention of making you respond. Why not telephone you or call around? Well it may be the case that we are not yet able to achieve direct face-to-face contact with you because of your implementation of No Contact. We choose not to telephone you because we want a message to be conveyed to you, say by text, e-mail or through a third party which means you have to respond to it. Should you do so we know that there is now a green light and we will easily be able to arrange a direct meeting with you. This is an elementary method of control that we deploy and one, which is used in order to test the water as to your amenability to establishing direct contact. It enables us to gauge how much effort and thus how much energy we will have to expend, in order to rope you back in. I mention this technique at the outset, as it will be applicable to many Power Plays and something you need to look out for.

This initial message, which seeks to hook you, will be along the lines of the following: -

"Please contact me ASAP - there is an emergency"

"Please call me as soon as you can, something awful has happened"

"We need to talk straight away - something has happened and you need to know"

Notice how the messages are not specific as to the reason why an emergency has arisen. This is also done on purpose. We know that one of your traits is the desire to know and therefore couched in such terms this message is designed to appeal to your need to know. It also plays on your sense of duty. If you ignore the message what might the repercussions be? What has happened and if you do not respond what could arise from it? There will be too many thoughts and combinations running through your mind along with the rising sensation of guilt if you do not reply. If you respond in the same or a similar manner to the way, we contacted you we will not provide any further details save underline the necessity of meeting. Accordingly, if you send a message back to us asking

"What is it? What has happened?"

We will not reply with chapter and verse. We will respond.

"Thanks for getting back to me. I really do need to see you. It is an emergency and it is too complicated to explain in a message."

You are already interested because of the way we framed the initial message. We have underlined the fact there is an emergency and you have responded. We will bounce messages back and forth until you agree to meet up. It is always the case that when I have used the emergency Power Play that the relevant victim has agreed to meet. Their sense of caring for others overrides any other concerns and thus I am afforded an audience. Once I am in front of you I commence with my best acting skills as I seek to convince you that some emergency or awful event has occurred. There will be three potential participants in this emergency. The first will be a fictitious friend or relative who has been involved in a car accident for example and I will feign my upset at this terrible turn of events and seek solace on your shoulder. I tend to only use the fictitious friend or family member if the other categories happened to have been used more recently. The fictitious person is naturally not someone you will have met. You therefore will have little empathy for this individual. I am reliant on your feeling concerned and sorry for me. If you have established No Contact, then your empathy levels will have been reduced towards me. I have to work hard to increase them using the fictitious friend. I usually lay on thick about how horrendous the accident was, how he has a wife and children and I need to do something to help them but I cannot think straight at present and so on. I will present myself as being in a tailspin in order to elicit sympathy from you. Once I have you hooked I will go to great lengths to stay with you since I am too upset to function away from you. The longer I can spend with you the greater the disruption there is to your No Contact and the greater the prospects of me Hoovering you back in. Once I am spending time with you I will use other Power Plays (e.g. Promise To Change) and apply my seductive flattery once again to Hoover you.

The second participant in this will be a Lieutenant who has been briefed beforehand. There is every chance that you will speak to or even go and see this Lieutenant and therefore the emergency is usually some kind of illness or disease that has a grip on my Lieutenant but one, which cannot be seen. Accordingly, mental illness, for example severe depression, is something that will be used or a recent diagnosis of cancer. Again I will be distraught at one of my good friends falling ill and look to you for support. The use of a Lieutenant is more effective as it provides corroboration for the yarn that I am spinning you.

The third participant is naturally me. Again, just like the Lieutenant I will opt for some unseen yet serious illness (which I will have spent some time researching and learning about in order to create authenticity in front of you). I might concoct a story about my job being on the line or that I am stressed at work and being bullied (oh the irony). There are various scenarios which I will have prepared and will readily roll out in front of you with lashings of woe is me in order to tap right into your sympathetic, empathic self. I have yet to find any empathic individual who has been able to resist such a performance. By gaining your attention once again (and thus with it fuel) I continue to worm my back in through seduction, additional Power Plays and ensuring I remain next to you so that No Contact has been truly smashed and my Hoover can then proceed without interference.

I do have to exercise caution with this Power Play however as if it used too often it will stretch credibility with even the most empathic person. After all, there are only so many distant grandparents who can pass away aren't there?

Should you implement No Contact and be faced by this Power Play you must ignore the overture. I know you will feel guilty and be thinking, "yes but what if something really has happened?" but consider just how coincidentally convenient this emergency is when you have just ended the relationship. You will be desperately unfortunate if the emergency turns out to be true. More likely than not it is a Power Play and the best way is to ignore the approach. Do not respond even to show sympathy as you are risking the activation of the mixture and this will give us encouragement. Do not respond even if your intention is to fact find to establish whether it is true. Again, by responding you are risking the mixture and the fact you have responded acts as encouragement to us and we will keep plugging away, pulling at those empathic heartstrings until you grant us an audience. Recognise this Power Play for what it is and ignore it.

8.2 Victim

This is a close cousin of the Emergency Power Play. It is designed to appeal to your empathic nature in order to bring you back to us. As usual we will look to control you by sending a message in order to hook you and then move to a personal audience to consolidate our position. You need to watch for messages such as

"This is terrible, I think something bad is going to happen, please let's speak."

"I didn't think you would do this and it has let me in pieces. Please speak to me before I go under."

"You and I need to speak, I don't know what else to do, I am lost without you, this hurts so much."

"Every second away from you is destroying me, please let's sort this out and talk, I am in a bad place."

Oddly enough there is an actual ring of truth to these messages. We are in a bad place because we have lost our primary source of fuel and we feel threatened by this. This creates urgency in us whereby we need to reinstate the supply of fuel and naturally we want this to be you. Our approach here again is to appeal to your need to know and most of all the fact that you care about people. We know that you will torment yourself when you consider the implementation of No Contact. Owing to the fact that you are a decent person you will want to do the right thing and also be seen to do the right thing. You will want to speak to us and explain why you are doing this. As I have explained above, you must not fall into this trap. We know that it will cause you considerable anguish by just implementing No Contact without conveying any message at all to us. That is why we respond with a Power Play such as the Victim approach. You will have worried (because you are such a selfless person) about the impact your cold-hearted and ruthless implementation of No Contact will have on us. You will be thinking that really you ought to speak to us, explain why you are doing it so we understand (in the same way that you would want to understand). We know you will have all of this running through your mind. Accordingly, the Victim Power Play will cater for this and show that the instigation of No Contact has truly hurt us. Yes, it has, for it has deprived us of fuel, but you will think that emotionally we have been injured and wounded by what you have done and you cannot stand to think that you have hurt someone. Even though we have subjected you to a sustained campaign of abuse the empathic traits that run so strong inside of you will be screaming at you to care, to fix and to heal. Given your weakened state and the lowering of your resistance (all caused by our manipulation of you) you will find it very difficult to resist the siren's call of this Power Play. It is during No Contact that you would do well to place some ice around that bleeding heart of yours because all of those traits that make you the good and decent person that you are will also prove to be your downfall. We know all about how empathic you are, that is why we chose you. Your empathy gave us fuel and your empathy is the key to reinstating that fuel.

Playing the Victim Power Play comes naturally to us because we maintain that we are the victims in all of this. The world is a cruel and a harsh place. It is uncaring. How can it be anything other than when it has consigned us to a lifetime of harvesting fuel? Of course, this is where we demonstrate the paradox that we are. On the one hand we will revel in the machinations in which we engage in so that we may harvest fuel. We will delight in wielding our Devil's Toolkit as we manipulate and push and pull.

We feel like a god wielding such power. Yet, in the next breath we will complain about how this never-ending quest for the acquisition of fuel is hard, tiring and unfair. We will ignore the inherent contradiction in those stances. Our stance is whatever we say or do which suits our purposes are the correct responses. If that changes week-to-week or even moment-to-moment, then so be it and there is nothing wrong with that. Playing the victim comes naturally to us. We see people out to topple us we regard you as the competition and the enemy. Why is that you try and move the spotlight away from us? Why do you not do what we want? It is all part of your scheme to do us down isn't it? You are colluding with the others to end my reign; I know it. You have sought to end our relationship after everything that I have done for you. Abuse? What abuse? I was trying to help you, show you the way and I only ever had your best interests at heart. You are so ungrateful. I do not know why I ever bothered trying to love you. You see how readily it flows from us. We are the victims in all of this and therefore playing up to that with a Victim Power Play comes to us as readily as breathing.

8.3 Threats

Intimidation is one of our manipulative tools and we will not shy away from using this device when it comes to trying to derail your attempt at No Contact. When we seduce you we do many thing and one of those things is the gathering of information about your weaknesses, your secrets, your fears and your vulnerabilities. We are adept at garnering information from you. This will be done under the auspices of helping you and apparently caring about you but it is nothing of the sort. This information is gathered for the purpose of stockpiling in our arsenal for later use against you. The intelligence we collect about your weaknesses will be used when we commence our devaluation of you. You will have given this information readily and now you find it is being used against you. The effect is devastating. We will also use this information we have when we are seeking to destroy your No Contact. It is something of a blunt instrument and again is likely to follow a two-stage process. Firstly, assuming we are able to convey the message to you, we will explain that unless you meet with us we will carry out some act. Usually this will be the dissemination of information about you, which exposes some secret, or weakness that you have. This can range from something which you find embarrassing and that you would rather other people did not know through to those secrets which could cause you trouble with family, friends, your employment and possibly even the authorities. Rest assured that we would have such information about you because we make it one of our missions to obtain it from you during the seduction stage. We want to do this because: -

1.   It makes us look like we care about you so that you will bind yourself closer to us; and

2.   It provides us with ammunition to use during devaluation and also to form part of the Threats Power Play when we are attacking your implementation of No Contact.

You have no chance to avoid this scenario because you will always willingly give this information to us during the seduction because at that juncture you have no idea what you have been ensnared by. Accordingly, unless you have lived liked a saint and have no weaknesses whatsoever we will have gathered this required information about you.

We will threaten to act or release this information about you. We may also threaten to carry out certain acts against you. The more advanced of our kind will not make such threats in a form which has been documented to avoid the risk that you will then use this threat against us. There are two main ways in which this can happen. You will show it to other parties such as family and friends as evidence of what you have to put up with. This damages our façade and may turn popular opinion against us. Secondly, certain of our threats may stray into the criminal domain. Threats to damage your property, hurt you or others close to you. In such circumstances, the more advanced of our kind will be careful only to utter such threats against you in person when there are no witnesses and it is only you and I there. Our threats are effective for three reasons: -

1.   If they are based on your weaknesses then you know them to be true and you fear those weaknesses being exposed to a wider audience;

2   If they are based on your secrets you will again know them to be true and you will fear exposure; and

3.   If they are based on causing you harm (outside of the above two categories) for instance beating you up or burning down your house, you know from the behaviour exhibited during devaluation that it is no idle threat and that we are perfectly capable of taking such a step.

Once we have used a threat to secure a meeting with you we may issue further threats and/or use additional Power Plays as we Hoover you back in. There is a high prospect of threats being used against you because we will always have information available about you. Furthermore, your despicable act in going No Contact means that our ignited fury will erupt through the declaration of threats as we seek to lash out against you by using our fury as a weapon.

The most effective way to deal with this Power Play is to put yourself in a position whereby you cannot receive the threat and we know we cannot convey it to you. That immediately defeats the Power Play. Of course attaining such a position is difficult. If we are able to convey the threat to you, you face a difficult decision. You cannot call our bluff. If you do not respond to our threat, then we will carry it out and therefore we will take a certain step and/or disseminate information about you. Alternatively, you take the dangerous step of agreeing to meet us and then you are at considerable risk of further Power Plays and being Hoovered because you have willingly breached No Contact. You are in an invidious position but in such a circumstance your need to defeat us should be the paramount consideration. Accordingly, the threat should be regarded as the lesser of the two evils and you will need to maintain No Contact and not respond to the first attempted threat. This will result in it being carried out. The first stage threat is unlikely to be a criminal act (unless we are low-functioning and if it is a criminal act then you have an immediate course of action available to you, subject to proof) and accordingly you will have to ride out whatever it is, possibly face a difficult time from people you know, even lose friends but that can be addressed at a later stage. The most important point for you is to maintain No Contact. With the Threat Power Play there is likely to be a cost to you but you should come to regard it as a price worth paying in order to escape our clutches.

8.4 The Spectre

This Power Play tends to be adopted in circumstances where we have time on our side. It may be that we are able to draw on our supplementary sources sufficiently whilst we engage in finding a new primary source and/or look to Hoover you back in. The Spectre Power Play does not rely on trying to get a message to you but it does require knowledge as to your whereabouts. This Power Play is used when we cannot get direct access to you but we know that we can be seen by you. We will use this Power Play when we know that you are of a nervous disposition. It also taps in to your desire to know. The premise is simple. Everywhere you go you will find us hanging around. We will position ourselves so that you can see us and we will just hang around. It might be waiting in the reception area of where you work or pacing up and down in the street outside. If there is the option of being able to engage with you, we will of course take it so this Power Play is used in circumstances where we can be seen but not heard. The intention behind it is to have you wondering what we are going to do. Are we going to try and get to you? Are we waiting for an opportunity to attack you? Why are we there? This not knowing will get to you and cause you considerable anxiety. If you send someone to ask us what we want, we will just explain we are waiting for someone else or walking past. That may satisfy the enquirer but we know it will not satisfy you. You know us well enough to understand that we are up to something and the fact we have not yet made our move will cause you considerable anxiety and distress. Day after day we will hang around like some spectre, doing nothing yet always begin there in order to spook you. On and on we will continue until it becomes too much for you to endure and you confront us.

It is likely that you will confront us in a heightened emotional state because our spectral campaign has got to you. This provides us with an instant hit of fuel and also allows us to seize the advantage because in your distress you will not be thinking straight. We will look to calm you down and reassure you that all we want to do it talk and straighten things out. You will be caught off-guard by the reasonableness of our response and accordingly will agree to do so. Now we are through the door and back in your face where we ill unleash additional Power Plays and apply our seductive charm once again so that we Hoover you in. By pushing you to a heightened emotional state and then offering a calm approach to you, we manage to pull you in once again.

Should you find this Power Play being used against you then the way to deal with it is to weather it. Eventually we will need fuel and therefore we will go to a different source or try a different technique to Hoover you. Whatever anxiety this technique may cause you, keep in mind it is just a small percentage of the anxiety you will suffer if you succumb to our overture. Get on with what you are doing on a daily basis and put our presence from your mind as best you can. If no threats are being made and we are just hanging around, then it is the Spectre Power Play and eventually we will drift away when we realise that it is having no effect on you.

Do not be tempted to try and involve the authorities against us for stalking you. We will be anticipating such a move and we know we have got to you (which will give us further fuel and encouragement). Remember that we are the charming and persuasive one and we will have little difficulty in persuading a law enforcement officer that we are not doing anything untoward and that is you being paranoid. We may even attempt to charm them to broker a meeting between us if we feel we can achieve this. Such a step will prove attractive to us because you will struggle to refuse a reasonable request from law enforcement to sit down and address one another in a calm environment. The approach you must adopt is to continue to ignore us. Creating a reaction is what we want.

8.5 Santa Claus

The Santa Claus Power Play is one whereby we will send you a present each and every day in the expectation that your resistance will crumble and you will engage with us. The beauty of this Power Play is that it can have one of two outcomes. On the one hand you may be won over by this expression of affection and largesse and want to thank us. On the other hand, you may confront us in order to tell us to stop sending the presents. Either way we have got you to engage with us and that is what it is all about.

This Power Play will be deployed when we know that you especially enjoy receiving surprises and that you have a material element to your make-up. Everybody likes to receive a gift. Everybody likes a pleasant surprise and therefore playing on this we will arrange for gift after gift after gift to be delivered to you. Again if you have managed to place yourself out of reach and sight then this Power Play will not work. Where we know of a place you will be, whether it is home, somewhere else you are staying, work or even a social venue you often frequent we will ensure that a gift is sent there. Similar to the methodology of sending a message this Power Play relies on getting you to respond and thus reacting to the assertion of our control. The advantage this Power Play is that it is premised on something pleasant. The gifts will be sent in a manner, which will not suggest that they have come from me. There will be no shiny wrapping but rather the standard brown box with the gift contained within. We will apply our minds to selecting those gifts, which are of considerable significance to you in the context of our relationship. It might include a particular CD of an artist we both listened to, a book we enjoyed reading, tickets to an event we enjoyed together and so on. This Power Play utilises elements of Ever presence in order to be effective in causing you to yield to this charm offensive. The gifts will have been carefully selected to cause a positive reaction in you and moreover in those who happen to be with you when you open it. Accordingly, if we are sending these gifts to your workplace or where you are staying with a friend we will be counting on them reacting favourably to them as well.

"Oh how sweet, he must really miss you if he has sent you that."
"Wow, that is beautiful, he obviously still loves you very much, perhaps you ought to speak to him?"
"That is amazing, I wish someone would buy me that, you are so lucky."

Comments such as these will prove helpful in reducing your willpower and pressuring you to engage with us. We will also use Lieutenants in the delivery of these goods if possible to bring about added pressure.

The gifts will range from the small and thoughtful to the expensive and impressive. Of course we will resent forking out our money in this manner but we will regard it as an investment in order to recover the fuel we so desperately need. Of course we will always be keeping in mind that in much the same way that a woman who marries for money earns every penny, that you will ultimately end up paying for these gifts. You need to keep such a thought in your mind and reject the gifts. As I have written above in the chapter addressing the steps you must take, organise for a gatekeeper who will intercept these gifts. They may keep them to one side and check whom they are from or best of all they will reject them and have them returned to sender. Letting these gifts through your gateway is perilous as the sustained drip drip effect will see us relying on your good nature. You will question your stance as these gifts show affection and love still for you and you of course always believe in love. It also pulls at your sense of decency and good manners. Surely you should at least thank us for the thoughtful gifts as it would be rude not to? This is what we are counting on. We rely on your decency and empathic qualities to erode your own No Contact and thus you will engage with us.

Once we are face to face you will be entering dangerous territory since we will be able to exert our considerable charm as we look to Hoover you back into our world and draw fuel from you once again.

Reject the gifts and put in place a gatekeeper who will not even tell you about them. This way you avoid activating the mixture, you send a clear message to us and you maintain No Contact by repelling this Power Play.

8.6 False Suicide

It is extremely rare for our kind to commit suicide. It does happen but it is very much the exception. The reason for this is that we have no desire to end our greatness. It tends to happen to those of our kind who have other co-morbid mental health issues. Ordinarily we are of the view that the world needs us and therefore why on earth would we remove ourselves from it? Of course this does not mean that we are above using the threat of suicide as a method to breach your No Contact. The False Suicide Power Play is a relative of the Emergency and Victim Power Plays. It is a powerful move on our part and is always destined to have the empathic individual come running so that we are able to engage with them. This act plays on the following: -

1.   Your desire to prevent harm;
2.   Your sense of guilt that you have caused us, the person you love, to end our life;
3.   The demonstration of our utter misery at being parted from you

All of these three things appeal greatly to your empathic traits and therefore will draw you in. In order to have maximum effect we do not use suicide as a threat. The Threat Power Play is all about the damage that will be done to you and not to us. We will use this Power Play as a means of telling you what is about to happen or has indeed happened. There will not be a message stating: -

"If you do not speak to me I will kill myself."
Instead you should expect messages such as
"I can no longer live without you. Good bye."

"There is nothing to live for now I have lost you. Farewell."

"I am broken beyond repair by losing you and have no longer any need to live. I love you."

This will create the impression that by the time you have got the message we have already committed suicide or the act is ongoing that very moment. This is entirely intentional. Rational thought will be cast aside and instead your response will be purely emotional. If this message was sent to us we would just shrug, regard you as an attention seeker trying to shift the spotlight onto yourselves and we would get on with seducing our new prospect. We have no longer any need for you and therefore do not care what you do. Heartless? Of course, but you know that is what we truly are. By contract, sending such a message to you presses all your empathic buttons and without any regard for whether it is a real message or not you will do your utmost to come and find us and satisfy yourself that we are alright. We will be counting on this and we will ensure you are able to find us. We will often use a lieutenant in these machinations that will know exactly where to find us. The Lieutenant will present in a state of urgency and explain that he or she has just received a message along the lines of one of the above messages and therefore you need to come quick and help. This ensures you are taken directly to me.

You will either find me feigning being distraught and sat there with a noose in our hands or the proverbial packet of pills and bottle of vodka nearby. We may even push it one step further for maximum effect and take a few of the pills and make ourselves appear woozy and out of it so you are particularly alarmed. There may even be a few half-hearted scratches at our wrists with a razor. All of it will be a sham but your appearance with concern writ large on your face will provide us with fuel and immediately we are through the gateway and presented with a golden opportunity to Hoover you back based on your gushing sympathy and empathy for us. We will act up so we appear ill in order to have you nurse us and thus by keeping you around and making you feel guilty we will work our charm on your once again.

How do you counter this? As ever if you are out of reach it cannot be used. If we can get a message to you and you receive one of this nature it will be very hard for you to resist. This is because it is a heightened emotional situation and one, which lends itself to an empathic person like you. In addition, the immediacy of the situation is designed to prevent you from thinking logically and causing you instead to react. You must bear in mind that it is extremely rare that a narcissist will take his or her life. In the vast majority of times it will be a device and no more. Accordingly, you are best served by ignoring it and recognising it for what it is. Your failure to respond will not tip us over the edge. We will try a different Power Play instead. This is a highly seductive method of getting you to respond and one you will have to exert considerable will power against in order to resist. If in the tiny cases the message is real and you do not prevent it happening, then yes you will be wracked with guilt but you still have rid of the narcissist haven't you? The difference is, someone like me can see it that way, you will find such a proposition horrendous even though you recognise the truth of such a comment and the ultimate benefit to you. You can take solace from the fact that it is extremely unlikely to happen. This Power Play, like so much we do, is based on pretence.

8.7 Sex

If you have read my book **Sex and the Narcissist** you will be aware of just how powerful a tool sex is when wielded by us. It will come as no surprise to you that this remains the case when we are seeking to disrupt No Contact. We are (save for the Victim Narcissist) accomplished in matters that take place between the sheets and this proves a highly addictive quality. Many victims of ours will often remark at how good the sex was, not all, but a lot do so. The sex we provide is based on extensive experience and delivered in a supercharged and heightened environment so that it is extremely memorable. This generates an addictive quality, which binds you to us quickly and tightly during the seduction. It also provides us with a means by which we can abuse our sexual brilliance to bring about highly effective devaluations. By the same token, the promise of the reinstatement of this sexual nirvana is a very enticing device, which can be wheeled out when we are trying to break your No Contact.

We may use it in the context of a message. Certainly during our seduction of you we would regularly prime you for a sensational sexual encounter with us by sending you a steady stream of suggestive and racy texts. This works well when you are being seduced. Sending a text of a sexual nature when you have instigated No Contact proves a riskier step. Viewed without the glow of seduction it takes on a different complexion and in such circumstances unless we are very sure that it is something you will respond to; it is rare that we will commence a Sex Power Play through conveying a message to you. Instead we will use some other means, a different Power Play to bring about a face-to-face engagement. It is then that we are much more likely to make a Sex Power Play as the very nature of the act relies on close proximity.

I recall with particular fondness doing this with a former girlfriend Karen. She had a vast sexual appetite and therefore my proficiency in bed was something, which she found highly attractive during the seduction and thereafter, when I took it away from her, something that caused her grave consternation. She wanted sex often and regularly and she regarded it as the ultimate expression of love between two people. Karen placed great stock in the sexual act. I have to concede that she was very good in bed and was amenable to new ideas and techniques. She was not afraid to initiate them either although I always delighted in blocking such attempts so she understood who was in control. I was always able to bring her to heel by using sex. She craved it, demanded it and placed great value in the fact that we coupled in this way. She made a rod for her own back in this regard.

On the one occasion that Karen decided that she had had enough and sought to end matters with me, I managed to engineer, through the use of a Lieutenant who I had placed in her camp, a meeting to try and iron matters out. I knew she had begun her No Contact (of course she did not call it that, in her eyes it was just the end of the relationship and she wanted nothing more to do with me) in a half-hearted manner because I knew she adored me and always wanted me but as ever the harshness of her devaluation had caused her to review matters. She sent me a message telling me it was over and not to contact her. I sprang into action and activated my Lieutenant to persuade her to meet me in order to sort out what was really troubling her. I knew by framing it in such a way she could not resist the opportunity to have her say and here I was generously providing her with a platform. I also suggested that meeting at a neutral venue would be sensible and I therefore made arrangements to meet her at a decent hotel in the city. Of course, in accordance with my view that every battle is won before it is fought, I ensured that I maximised my chances of Hoovering her back to me by deciding that a Sex Power Play would be the key to success. I also had established that the meeting appeared to be on neutral ground when in reality it would be taking place on my terms. Instead of meeting her in one of the hotel's bars or restaurants I booked a suite and then sent her a message telling her to go to the Suffolk Suite at 7pm.

At the appointed time I arranged myself and waited. She was punctual and there came a knock at the door at 7pm and I called out for her to come in. She did and stepped into the impressive suite. I was laying on the king size bed. Karen walked in and she had made an effort, as I knew she would. She looked fantastic. I smiled at her and then moved my eyes to indicate to the bed. I knew she would not be able to resist. Whenever we had cause to fall out during our relationship I knew the easiest way to surmount any anger or resistance on her part and bring her back under my control was to bed her. I would walk towards her and declare,

"I am taking you to bed."

It was like some hypnotic power word and she was powerless to resist. Alternatively, I would steer her into the bedroom and push he onto the bed whispering to her,

"I have to have you now."

All of her threats to depart and leave would evaporate as she would make a noise like a purr and immediately yield to me. Every single time I did this she immediately yielded to my control. It was highly effective and I wished it worked with all of my relationships. Still, I knew that it would work now and as my eyes indicated to the bed and then back to her I saw that smile I knew so well and within seconds she had joined me and we were kissing. A bout of athletic love-making followed and at its conclusion as we both lay there sated I turned to her and said,

"You cannot leave that can you?"

I could see she was trying to say no but her eyes betrayed her and eventually she gave the answer I wanted.

"No. I can't."

Thus she was mine once again and the flow of fuel was awesome.

Where we know that sex (and by its combining with love) is important to you, we will use sex as a Power Play to win you back. The addictive qualities of sex with us will prove extremely hard for you to resist. Once we have you in an environment where we are face-to-face and able to engage in sexual congress you are walking on thin ice. In order to avoid the risk of a Sex Power Play being used against you, you will need to ensure that you do not allow a face-to-face meeting to occur. Beware of Power Plays being used in conjunction to achieve your Hoovering. We may use an Emergency Power Play to send a message and secure the face-to-face meeting and thereafter once we are with you deploy a Sex Power Play. It is rare to see the Sex Power Play as the initial hook and therefore to negate this Power Play avoid any direct face-to-face engagement.

8.8 The Promise to Change

This Power Play is one, which always sucker the empathic individual. You believe that we can change and that somehow we can be fixed. You love nothing more than being the angel that saves us form ourselves somehow and fixes us. We are well aware of this and as a consequence we devise one of our Power Plays to cater for this need in you. Accordingly, we will recognise our failings and issue our promises to change. It might be promising to do things differently, sitting down and drawing up a list of alternative behaviours, agreeing to seek professional help or go to some form of counselling together. Whatever form it takes this Power Play will involve the recognition that we have done something wrong and the need and the appetite for change. Naturally it is all a sham.

I had this situation arise with Olivia, a former girlfriend and she of the magnificent legs. We never lived with one another, the relationship never veered towards doing so although I did try and get her to commit to doing so. She lived across the city from me, maybe twenty minutes away. I had not heard from her all day, which was slightly unusual, but I was not altogether perturbed by this, not since I was also trying to acquire a pa from the office as a new source of fuel. I was driving home and decided I would call Olivia on the hands free. The number rang and rang until her voicemail kicked in. I tried five more times and on each occasion the result was the same. This failure to answer her 'phone was now concerning me. I pulled over and sent a couple of text messages to her before I set off heading for home. There was no response to my enquiry and therefore I changed direction and headed to the apartment block where she resided to find out what was going on. I parked up and headed into the lobby of the expensive building. The concierge was sat behind his desk.

"Good evening Mr Tudor," he smiled in greeting. He knew me from numerous visits I had made and he opened the doors that allowed access to the building's lifts. I entered the lift and made my way to the fifteenth floor. I walked along the empty corridor until I reached Olivia's apartment and using the key she had given me, admitted myself into her home. I could hear a television and she was singing gently to herself as I walked into the open plan living area, the city beyond, a sea of lights and reflections off the glass and steel.

"What are you doing here?" she asked as she looked up from where she was stood preparing some vegetables in the kitchen area.

"I have been ringing you and you have not answered," I remarked with a hint of irritation.

She set the knife down and regarded me calmly.

"I know. I did not answer because I do not want to see you anymore. I had hoped my silence would speak for itself and you would have the decency to leave me alone, especially after the way you have treated me."

"Why?"

She sighed.

"Where do I begin? Could it be the systematic abuse that you have subjected me to over the last five months? You conned me HG. You made me think you were the one and then you changed and became a monster. I could not fathom it out. Why had this loving and charming man become this awful creature that shouts at me, criticises and belittles me, a man who now spends his time finding new and inventive ways to upset me?"

I stood listening. I had never seen her like this before. There was steel to her voice and an icy composure about her as she stood and reeled off a litany of abuses that I had apparently delivered to her. She recounted them in a calm and measured tone as if she was placing an order with a waiter in a restaurant. There was no anger, no resentment or upset. She stood and said her piece as I listened dumbfounded. She really meant all of this. I could not find any spark to ignite my fury. There was nothing and I could feel myself falling. The darkness was seeking to engulf me and I was unable to bring any anger or rage to bear against her. How had she done this? How had she managed to neutralise such an effective power? The awful realisation kicked in. She was discarding me, casting me coolly aside without a hint of emotion. There was only one thing for it.

"Please, please don't do this. I know I have not been as good a boyfriend as I should have been. I am so so sorry. I know you don't deserve to be treated badly; it is just, I don't know, something seems to be wrong with me. I have barely slept for the last month and this has exhausted me. I think this is why I have been harsh with you. I feel lost and I do not know what to do about it. You know me, I am too proud to seek help, but as I have lain there in the dark, the room seeming to close in on me, I have known that something is very wrong but I do not know what. I am frightened Olivia, I think I am losing my mind," I said and then I let the first tear appear as I managed to squeeze it from my right eye. I summoned up every injustice I could recall. I reached for the sense of loss surrounding Amanda from all those years ago and then the anguish rose enabling me to turn on the waterworks. Thank God I had learned how to do that. The tears spilled down my cheeks as I sank to the expensive seat nearest to me. I buried my head in my hands, letting my low sobbing drift through the room. Seconds passed and then a hand alighted on my shoulder and pulled me into her embrace.

"Sssh, HG, I had no idea about this, come on, please don't cry, talk to me, I am sure we can sort this out," her soft words had lost the steel now.

"I need you to help me Olivia, only you can save me," I muttered through my hands.

"I will HG, I will," she soothed as her long limbs wrapped about me, cosseting me and comforting me. I gave another sob for effect but I knew I had got her back.

8.9 Appetite for Destruction

Unleashing a destructive tendency is one way of Hoovering you back in. This tends to be a violent and shocking Power Play, which will cause a knee-jerk reaction. In a way it is similar to the False Suicide because the effect will be to have you react in an emotional way without pausing for thought or consideration. By drawing you into our sphere of influence as you race to prevent us smashing things up, you will then be exposed to us so we can administer a further Power Play and roll out our seductive charm in order to Hoover you.

I once shared a home with Alex. You may recall that she was gymnast. I owned the property but she lived there with me, having sold her own house and deposited the funds in her bank account for an as yet undefined later use. It was a Thursday and when I returned from work I found that she was not there but a note was left in clear view on the occasional table in the living room.

"Dear HG, I have had enough. I do still love you but I cannot live with you. I have moved out. Please do not contact me until I have had time to recover. I will make arrangements to collect the rest of my possessions. Alex xxx"

I crumpled the note up in the palm of my hand as the fury rose inside of me. How dare she? How dare she walk out like this after all the things that I had done for her. The flames of my anger grew and rose, surging up inside as I found myself twisting left and right looking for a way to vent my rage. A torrent of abuse spilled from my lips as I became consumed by my anger. This woman had insulted me with her departure. She had not even had the decency to tell me to my face, after all the support I had given her, letting her live with me and shuttling to and from her gymnastic competitions. The ungrateful bitch. My sense of injustice was huge and with the firmest of reasons for feeling that way.

I marched over to the sideboard where her numerous trophies were displayed and picked up the largest. I twisted and pulled at the plastic until it snapped and then grabbed the next one. I bent it and then hurled it to the floor. A third trophy was selected and I dented the metal with my fists as I pounded it. I worked my way through all of her trophies, snapping, breaking and pummelling as my animated self was reflected in the mirror on the wall. Had I stopped to look at myself I would have seen the mask of hatred that was pulled tight across my face. I made my way into the garden. It was a summer evening and I made a fire in the brazier at the end of the garden before returning to the living room. I snatched up two of the largest trophies, now mangled and misshapen and hurled them into the flames and watched as the plastic began to melt, the metal started to blacken and the wood caught fire.

I returned to the house and made for the bookcase. I hauled all the books that belonged to her from the bookcase and took them to the brazier. I tore each book down its spine as I imagined I was tearing Alex in two, before dropping the rent apart novel into the orange flames. Two pictures that she loved were next. I took a knife to them slashing them and then hanging them back up. She could look on them when she tried to recover them. I surged up the stairs and into our bedroom. I flung open the wardrobe and found many of her clothes had already been moved, but still some remained. Like a dervish, I assaulted the suits and dresses, slashing at them with the knife in my hand, as if I was stabbing and slashing Alex. The garments, now shredded and in ribbons hung from the rail or slipped forlornly to the floor. I scooped up some shoes and took them outside and added them to the flames. Back in the bedroom I opened the drawers on the nightstand and rifled through to find she had not taken her passport. I shoved that into my suit pocket. I decided I would keep that to use as leverage.

I made my way to the bathroom and found that most of her toiletries had been removed, but of those left they were emptied into the sink, their contents squeezed from them and the perfume bottles smashed on the tiled floor leaving an overpowering cloud of scent as the contents leaked across the tiles. I stormed into the study and noticed she had taken her laptop and her tablet but she had not touched the PC, which belonged to me. I switched it on and as I broke another picture she liked over her knee I began to delete the pictures she had stored on the PC. I entered the kitchen and grabbed the scales she used to measure out her food as part of her fitness regime. I found a hammer from under the sink and smashed and dented the scales with the hammer. Opening a cupboard, I saw her favourite mug and that was hurled to the floor so it shattered on the ground. My eye fell on the champagne flutes that she liked. We had bought them together but she liked them so one by one I cast them onto the ground as the glass fractured and broke. Next was a set of plates she had picked. I bought them but they could go next, the crockery smashing and spilling across the floor as I slammed them downwards. I could always buy more plates.

Still my anger raged as I prowled back and forth through the house looking for anything that she owned or liked which I could consign to the inferno outside or smash under the hammer that I wielded. Perhaps an hour later I say at the base of the stairs, my chest rising and falling from the exertion, the product of my destruction lying all around, the smell of smoke drifting in from the garden. I pulled out my phone and began to record all of the carnage, the ripped clothes, the shattered utensils, the battered trophies and the still burning books before I sent the video to her number and then I was finally able to smile as the surge of power took over from the burning rage.

I was not content with smashing up and destroying Alex's possessions for her treachery. Once I had finished deleting the various photos and some art projects she had stored on the PC I went online and used the passwords I had acquired to cause some further havoc. I accessed her Facebook account and sent various messages to certain men I knew she was friendly with in order to provide me with material to use against her. I sent certain flirtatious messages, posted overly-friendly comments on pictures and added a few choice photographs on to her profile that she would not have liked to have had put there. Taking this step would provide me with two purposes. The first was that I had material to turn to people and show how horribly she had behaved towards me. This would certainly diminish any sympathy they felt towards her when she arrived with her tales of woe about me. Furthermore, it would make people feel sorry for me. Secondly, it meant I had something to berate her with in order to bring her back to me through emotional blackmail. Of course I was careful to delete evidence of this on the PC. I am far more tech savvy that her.

She also made the error of leaving in her nightstand drawer her emergency credit card. I knew that she did not carry it with her to avoid the temptation to spend on it. Instead, she kept it hidden away to use should there be some emergency. It was evident that she had forgotten it. I took the opportunity to go on a spending spree. I ordered some sex toys in her name and sent them to her work and her parent's address. I sent pizzas to all the neighbours. I booked a break for me in a fortnight's time. I also ordered a succession of self-help books and analysis books dealing with Borderline Personality Disorder and sent them to her sister's address. That made me laugh as I thought how that would certainly kick the hornet's nest between the two of them. I also: -

1. Bought jewellery for two prospects I was pursuing;
2. Replaced the crockery that I had smashed up;
3. Bought tickets to various shows which I then gave away to my junior colleagues receiving a delicious burst of admirable fuel in the process;
4. Organised a funeral wreath bearing her name to be sent to her parents' house;
5. Purchased a painting I had wanted as a little reward for my inventive and hard work.

The upshot of her leaving such an item in my possession was that she incurred a rather large shock when the credit card bill arrived which followed on from the various fallouts that arose from the transactions that I had engaged in. Not only did she want the money back (which was not an issue of being able to reimburse her, more whether I chose to – I chose not to) but she was inflamed by what I had bought and what had arisen from those purchases. She could not help herself but return to the house and confront me. Once I had her back I was able to soak up all that marvellous fuel she was pouring my way and then engage in unfurling the rest of my plan, now that she had put herself in my sights once again, to make her remain with me. I knew precisely which buttons to press with Alex and once I had ensured she had come to confront me I was able to wrap my tendrils about her.

The simple choices which face you when faced with such destruction are allow it to happen, stay away and if you feel it appropriate bring criminal charges against us. There may be sentimental objects amidst everything we destroy and we may also cause you financial chaos but the alternative to trying to prevent all of this happening is to expose yourself to confronting us and in turn risk being Hoovered. Items can be replaced, they will be insured in all likelihood and ultimately you ill need to place your sanity and welfare above that of inanimate objects. Not something we ever did.

8.10 The White Knight

This Power Play is to a large extent the polar opposite of the Victim Power Play. On this occasion we recognise that you will be upset and distressed by what has happened, by feeling the need to leave us and no doubt putting yourself in a difficult position across a number of fronts. You may be in temporary accommodation, you may face financial difficulties, be away from your family and friends. We will have this worked out already and indeed we will have engineered some if not all of these difficulties that you now find yourself in as a consequence of firstly your involvement with me and secondly (and this is what we will focus on) your implementation of No Contact. When we first seduced you, we looked to be the white knight that comes riding to your rescue. Invariably, because of the conditioning that society subjects people to and in particular women, there still remains the concept of the damsel in distress being liberated by the knight in shining armour. Of course this is an insult to all the independent, secure and self-sufficient women who are successful and fulfilled in many aspects of their lives. I however need not be troubled with whether they feel insulted or offend by this indoctrination because there remains a significant part of the female population that subscribes either consciously or sub-consciously to this ideal. Consequently, the concept of the arrival of the white knight on his charger is a concept, which lends itself to my seduction of you. Having used this as part of my campaign of love-bombing once and thus imbued inside of you the image of how I am here to help and rescue you, allied with my knowledge that you want to be rescued and protected, I know that deploying such a technique when you are trying to effect No Contact is likely to meet with success.

This Power Play is not suited to all of our kind as often it needs to be deployed with someone who has access to resources and the lower functioning of our brethren are likely to be excluded from this. In order to use this Power Play, we will come riding to the rescue, resplendent on our horse, armour shining and lance tilted ready to slay the dragon which plagues you (no not ourselves!). This will manifest through

- Depositing money in your bank account
- Arranging accommodation for you, say at a hotel or a rented property
- Organising child minding
- Arranging transport for you
- Attending to administrative matters on your behalf
- Catering for medical issues

Choose any issue which may be causing you some consternation and at the outset of No Contact we will suddenly appear having addressed the issue on your behalf. This step is taken in order to tap into your natural gratitude at having had a difficult situation resolved or made less onerous. We expect you to express your thanks because you have been brought up to do so and behave politely. We recognise you will feel relief and that you will wish to express your thanks as a consequence of this relief and also the need to avoid seeming churlish by expressing your gratitude to us. It is all about creating a debt, which you feel you, will have to discharge by getting in contact with us. We may often take the step without even attempting to tell you that we are doing it. In such circumstances if you then contact us to express your thanks we know that we have been able to exert control over you once more. We will then exploit this by asking if there is anything else we might help you with and suggesting we meet to resolve matters both between us and those matters, which have arisen as a consequence of our behaviour and your departure. We create this debt and make you feel obliged to cater for it. In the same way we gave you so much during our seduction and then made you pay for it during the devaluation we are doing the same here. This Power Play is another form of manipulative seduction.

In order to deal with this, accept the assistance. Why not? It was freely given and after all we most likely put you in that difficult position but do not express any gratitude. Consider it compensation for everything that you have endured. Feel no sense of obligation towards us as a consequence of this apparent generosity and instead see it as the least that could be done for you after everything else that we have inflicted against you. By altering your mindset you will feel less obliged to express gratitude and accordingly you will lessen the risk of being Hoovered by us.

8.11 False Criminal Allegations

This is a relative of the Threat Power Play because we are threatening to proceed with a criminal complaint against you. It does not matter that there is only our word to support it, this will at least result in an investigation and your likely arrest. This will cause you anxiety and upset and we will embellish the details, rope in a Lieutenant to support our false complaint and ensure that you have the prospect of humiliation at best and incarceration at worst hanging over you. The Greater Narcissist usually takes this step as it is a particular malicious step to take which has no regard at all for the truth of the matter, not the actual consequences which may arise for us by making a false complaint. Of course we do not care about those consequences because they will not apply to us. We will be able to talk our way out of them as we can with everything.

The intention of this Power Play is to use the criminal agencies to locate you and obtain that information for our use. It is then to put you under pressure and generate anxiety for you. The prospect of a criminal conviction may have ramifications for you concerning your employment (thus we attack another support network in this manner), it will support our character assassination of you by convincing your supporters that you are the trouble maker and it will seek to cause them to switch their allegiance to me instead. Ultimately it is designed to flush you out so you contact us and plead for us to do the right thing to drop the complaint against us. We will of course grant you an audience for the purposes of trying to persuade us to change our mind and do the decent thing and drop the complaint. You will feel angered by this injustice but you will come to us showing humility and contrition because you know that is what we want to see. This of course amounts to all good fuel for us and enables us to exert control again over you. Naturally we will be content to drop the complaint and explain how it was all a mistake or how we have reconciled our differences and no longer wish to proceed with the case. We will not do this however until we know we have pulled you back in to our sphere of influence. We will listen to you at the first meeting and tell you that we will consider what you have to say and come back to you. We will make you wait and sweat some more before meeting you again. We will tussle with you over details as we extract more fuel from you and continue to increase your desperation and anxiety. We will then shift the topic of the discussion to you and me and little by little, using those salami-slicing tactics for which we are famous we will bring you back under our spell and once that has finally been achieved we will consent to the dropping of the complaint. By that time, you have been Hoovered back in, grateful that it is all over and basking in the false golden period which we have reinstated as your "reward" for returning to us.

How might you deal with this? You have no option other than to defend yourself and fight it. No matter what we have accused you of do not be tempted to trade your No Contact for the removal of the complaint. It will be difficult as you may find yourself facing a serious accusation and with our accomplices supporting our version of event your prospects may seem slim. However, you need to fight the complaint. It is unlikely that we will back down and you will have to hope that the prosecuting authority decides against proceeding with it or you are acquitted at trial. This may sound like a considerable risk but naturally within the context of such a case and properly advised by a competent lawyer there is much you can do to increase your chances of forcing the no further action of the complaint or being acquitted. Similarly, fight fire with fire and notify the authorities of the transgressions of your narcissist. There are likely to be some. This may prove sufficient pressure to cause the narcissist to back down and if it does not it is likely to pollute his credibility in your case. This Power Play calls into play high stakes but consider whether you wish to go back to the nightmare of our false reality and all that that entails or whether you wish to preserve No Contact and try to escape our grip. This Power Play is a difficult one to deal with because such complaints can take on a life of their own but you can challenge it and you must keep in mind that the alternative is being ensnared once again and that is what you must avoid at all costs.

8.12 All Points Broadcast

You can expect to find this Power Play used against you when we have our alternative primary source lined up. In such circumstances you will have been very close to a discard but by implementing No Contact you have got in there first and naturally this criticism of us will ignite our fury. We have no pressing need to recover you as a fuel source because we have already seduced a new one, but that will not stop us from wanting to punish you and of course there is always the attraction of obtaining Hoover fuel from you.

The All Points Broadcast is done as a form of triangulation. You may have instigated No Contact but we take this step in the anticipation of some form of information reaching you. It may arise from us messaging you, it most likely will occur from a third party telling you and/or it may arise if you are foolish enough to engage in stalking our social media profiles. With this Power Play we will create a deluge of announcements, an avalanche of photographs and repeated declarations of our new love. We will take each and every opportunity to be photographed in all the places we took you to so that should you check our social media profiles you will find her and I smiling out at you looking the very picture of happiness and contentment. I will announce future trips with the new object of my affection, which of course will be linked, to places we went to our you wanted to go to. We know that you cannot stand it when someone else comes along. No matter how much you may feel antipathy towards us the fact that someone else is now enjoying that (supposed) love and the golden period causes you concern. You try and tell yourself that it will not be long before she finds out the truth about us. Eventually she will be subjected to the hell that you endured but then comes that creeping and nagging doubt. What if this time it is different? What if she somehow manages to tame us (after all you are the eternal believer in the fact that we can be healed)? How about if he has changed and they are happy together? You will have missed out on that opportunity after everything you and I have been through together. He cannot love her in the way that he loved me, it is too early for that. We had something special didn't we? All of these thoughts will be tumbling through your mind, pulling at you and undermining your resolve. You will start to think that if you cannot be with me then she should not either and you will warn her off. You will let her know what a bastard I really am. You will tell her everything and tell her to run to the hills. Of course she will not listen. I have already primed her to be wary of my crazy ex. I have already reeled off all the awful things, which you did to me as I play an early pity card with her. She will not believe anything you say as you will be tainted with jealousy and she will not believe any ill of this charming, wonderful man who loves her so perfectly (sound familiar at all?) Of course this is what I am hoping you will do. I am hoping that you will break cover to speak to her and thus this will enable me an opportunity to speak with you. Once I have secured this opportunity I will point out I did not realise just how much you cared for me still and intertwined with this Power Play I will unleash a Promise to Change Power Play as well to maximise the pressure on you. I will explain how the new prospect does not mean as much to me but you devastated me when you ended things. Of course I am conveniently ignoring the fact that I had been cultivating the new lady as a prospect when I was seeing you as well but I am not going to let that detail stand in the way of Hoovering you. The charm will be laid on thick as I Hoover you back in with empty promises. You will cave in because you want to get one over on the new prospect and you also want to have another chance to experience the golden period and make things right. The opportunity to do this is too great to resist. I will soon have you back with me and enjoying a brief golden period but I will not have let go of the new prospect either and it will not be long before I am triangulating the pair of you, drinking deep of the fuel that I will obtain from this manipulation of you both. I am content to do this in the fullness of time but most of all I am relishing the Hoover fuel that is pouring from you because I have managed to ensnare you again by causing you to feel jealous of

133

somebody else. If you analyse your reaction in the cold light of day, it will make no sense but then nothing does with me. It is all about the emotion and an emotional creature such as you is motivated by the prospect of rekindling that perfect love once again and moreover ensuring that nobody else has access to it. It is your as because you are a fixer, you want it to work.

To overcome this Power Play, you must not have any regard to any content contained within the APB. Most certainly you must not (as outlined above) trawl my social media and run the risk of the mixture being activated. Recognise this crowing for what it is and be thankful that I have found a new primary source of fuel so quickly. This means you are likely to be left alone sooner. Fight the desire to want the golden period again. Remember that what the new prospect is experiencing is precisely what happened to you and you know where that ended up. Nothing will change. Nothing will be different and you do not owe it to her to warn her. You must look to your own defences, ignore the APB Power Play and focus on maintaining No Contact.

8.13 The Grand Gesture

This Power Play has similarities to the Santa Claus Power Play but it is based on one salvo. Admittedly it is a powerful salvo, which is designed to wow you just as we did when we seduced you. You should by now be noticing that there is a pattern of behaviour emerging. Many of these Power Plays will have been used (although not all) when we first seduced you and now they are being rolled out again. This is because the Hoover is in fact a further seduction of you but with a different complexion because you have experienced the hell of devaluation.

With the Grand Gesture we will select something we know that you enjoy very much such as a special event (a concert which it will be difficult to obtain tickets for) or an exotic holiday in a place you have always wanted to visit. It might be buying you a new car or paying for plastic surgery. We may even go so far as to propose marriage to you based on how much we need you. Whatever it is the Grand Gesture will exhibit our largesse and be focussed on something we know you want very much. The Grand Gesture will be unveiled in a way so that other people know about it so they will remark about how wonderful it is and in turn put you under pressure to accept it. In a similar way to the presents that are sent to you so that others witness their arrival and opening, the Grand Gesture is designed to impress not only you but also other people. Of course this appeals to our sense of showing off but it also enables us to harness their approval and delight to put you under pressure to accept.

We will find a way of ensuring the Grand Gesture is brought to your attention. A car may be left outside your office or home with a huge bow around it. The tickets may turn up with a courier who will stay until they are signed for ensuring that they reach your hand. If we decide that a marriage proposal is required we will organise the situation so that it attracts maximum publicity and demonstrates just how committed I am to your fuel, I mean to you. All of this is designed to appeal to that part of you that has always wanted to do the very thing that is now being dangled under your nose. It also appeals to your sense of decency by making you realise just how much we think of you that we would go to all this trouble. Surely this is evidence of contrition on our part and a desire to make good what has gone before? As ever we know you will be looking to find the good in us and a Grand Gesture is our way of magnifying this supposed good so it is in your face and not something you can miss.

The simple way to deal with the Grand Gesture is to decline it. Do not be concerned about causing offence, think on at the many offences we have caused you. Do not be influenced by what others may say but do not accept it. People are likely to comment adversely but they do not know what you know and in time they will and even if they do not, it does not matter. You must resist this one off blast from us and turn away from it to maintain No Contact.

8.14 Lieutenants

Lieutenants are a crucial element in my mission to obtain fuel. I have always a set of loyal Lieutenants who are recruited from different areas of my life thus allowing me to extend my reach influence. The Lieutenant must be at all times obedient, unquestioning and prepared to assist. It usually helps to have some kind of hold over them, which I do, although I need not go into explaining what those are for the purposes of this publication. Lieutenants are used to assist me in my manipulation of my targets and victims and also in effecting a Power Play to Hoover you back. The placement of Lieutenants is important and also the fact that you have no awareness as to whom they might be. This enables me to gather intelligence so that my Power Play is effective and swift in its application.

I had a girlfriend called Alex. She was a talented gymnast and she often railed against me but I managed to keep her under control, after all, it is what I am good at. Alex once upped and left me without any warning. This caused me to unleash an orgy of destruction, which I will tell you more about in one of the Power Plays below.

Before Alex disappeared on that occasion of the destruction, she had tried to depart on two previous occasions. In fact, I reached the conclusion that the fairly hurried nature of her departure with her leaving most of her possessions behind was as a result of her desire to escape and the fact her previous plans had failed and been frustrated by me. On the two previous occasions, she had engaged in a greater degree of planning, but these plans were halted because she confided in the wrong people. She chose to involve people in helping her leave me, who were loyal to me and also briefed to report to me any such behaviour.

The first time she made the mistake of seeking the assistance of one of my friends. He is a lawyer and is a friendly fellow who always made time for Alex and they got on very well. I suspect he had a soft spot for her but that was dwarfed by his obligation to me arising out of an incident which if brought to the attention of the relevant authority would have seen him struck off. Thus he was always going to do what I wanted. He was instructed to get close to Alex and keep me informed about what she got up to. He naturally obliged. When she went to him for some advice about the division of certain investments we had made jointly in one of my companies, she let slip that she was looking to exit the relationship. As soon as she had left his conference room he was on the 'phone to me. I was able then to prevent her departure by contacting her immediately and asserting my charm to remove her desire to leave me and implement No Contact. Alex had proved his worth to me by tipping me off and allowing me to intervene.

On the second occasion she made mention of her intentions to one of her friends, Rebecca. I had enjoyed a drunken romp with Rebecca and I threatened to tell Alex about it. At first she called my bluff, thinking that I was just as implicated in the infidelity so that I would not say anything to Alex. Of course, I knew that my manipulative hold on Alex was such that I would be able to twist the truth and show it was Rebecca who was the problem and thus she would end the friendship. I used my charm and intelligence to convince Rebecca that she would be the loser unless she helped me out and she agreed. Alex thought she could trust her friend when she asked her to help support her departure from me. All Rebecca did was inform me, admittedly through her self-pitying tears, but once again I had the upper hand and was able to launch a charm offensive to prevent Alex from executing her plan.

These are just two instances where I have been able to use Lieutenants. In these cases, they were used to supply with me the information that Alex was looking to leave and thus implement No Contact. I was forewarned and therefore able to apply a Power Play to my advantage. Sometimes the Lieutenant will be used as part of the Power Play itself for instance in conveying a message to the person seeking to implement No Contact or the Lieutenant engineers a situation whereby I am able to meet the person I am Hoovering when they though they had managed to keep me at arms' length. Once I am in the personal proximity of this person I will not relent until they have returned to me. You would do well to heed that point and ensure where you can that the narcissist in your life is not afforded an opportunity to address you face to face. Be wary of those you involve in your plans and consider that the very people who you think you can trust may well be one of my Lieutenants. My tendrils reach all over. When you are engaged in planning your departure and thereafter the maintenance of No Contact you should consider using those people who have never interacted with me. Establish who they are and where possible use them as part of your support network as there is every chance they will not have been tainted by my approach and therefore they will not be one of my Lieutenants. No matter how much you may think a person is loyal to you, if they have had interaction with me, there is a distinct chance I will have recruited them or at least tried to. I am the master manipulator and I will bring them alongside me to assist me over you. Do not think that a long-standing friend or family member is immune to becoming one of my Lieutenants and thus helping me with my Power Plays, they are not.

8.15 Mother of My Children

I have mentioned at an earlier stage in this book that effecting No Contact when you and the narcissist have children together makes No Contact extremely difficult. It can be done if it is deemed the right thing for the narcissistic parent not to have any contact with the children but that is a rare occurrence. Nevertheless, if you have children with a narcissist and feel you are able to instigate No Contact you can expect that they will be used as pawns in order to break No Contact and one way will be the Mother of my Children Power Play.

In this we will once again tug at your empathic traits. Whilst we could talk about wanting to see our children, how we might berate you for trying to take them away from us and such like, we know that you are likely to be immune to this and see it as a cynical ploy. Your empathic nature will be stronger towards the children than us and therefore if we try to use them as the reason for breaking No Contact you will want to shield and protect them. Accordingly, if we demand to see them and accuse you of being a wicked mother for preventing us from seeing them, we know we will only heighten you resolve to remain in a No Contact state. The children are a useful device to us and one which we will utilise because ultimately we only care about ourselves but as you have come to learn we will trample on and use anybody else in order to achieve our aims. Thus we will not make demands concerning the children but we will still prey on your empathic nature. We will focus on the connection that we have and that fact is that we have children together. We will acknowledge that as mother to our children, those very things that we hold most dear and precious (we know all the things to say to make us appear like we care) you hold a sacred role and we could not bear to be parted from you. We will laud you for the sterling role you have performed in their upbringing and apologise for any shortcomings we may have in this respect. Such apologies easily trip from our tongues. All of this is designed to point out that we cannot fall out with the mother of our children, it is not right and we both need to resolve our differences. This is a clever slant, which uses the children but in a way does not use them. We involve them but the focus is on your status as a mother. What we are also applying is a degree of reverse psychology. By emphasising your role as a mother we are reminding you that we are the father and although we do not say it, we are inferring that in the same way we cannot bear to fall out with the mother of our children then surely you do not want to fall out with the father of your children. We hope that for the sake of the children and recognising our roles and obligations to them (even though we have been curiously absent in that regard on many occasions) you will not want to maintain this hiatus. By heaping on the emotional pressure surrounding the children we will pull at your emotions so you eventually sit down and discuss matters with us. Once that happens we will continue to apply pressure and charm as we seek to Hoover you back in. We may continue with this Power Play or involve another also, so long as we achieve our aim.

Be wary of our intentions and your emotional response when it comes to the matter of children. Recognise that this is a last ditch attempt by us and where have we been in the past when you needed help and support with the children? Nowhere to be seen. Why has that now changed? Simply because we fear the permanent loss of our fuel as you instigate No Contact. Additionally, dependent on their ages, we may also fear the loss of the fuel that we obtain from our children too. Remember to us fuel is all that matters and therefore no matter what we may say with regards to your status as the mother of our children it is nothing more than another ruse and one which you must ignore.

8.16 I Can't Live Without You

This Power Play is a cousin of the False Suicide Power Play but there is no threat or execution of a false suicide bid but rather this protestation of being unable to live without you is a calculated trip down memory lane in order to invoke all of those delicious, wonderful thoughts and feelings we once shared at the outset of the relationship when we seduced you and put in place the golden period. By stressing how much we cannot live without you and then reminding you of all the marvellous things we have done together, the happy times we spent as a couple and such like I am actually saying to you,

"Do you think that you can live without me?"

Each time I mention that special occasion I am reinforcing that by doing what you are doing you are denying us the opportunity of making more delicious and long standing memories. I will conveniently brush over my devaluing treatment of you because I do not regard it as relevant here. Instead I will trot out a list of the special memories that we have created because I know that is what you want more than anything else. You want to be able to wave a magic wand and return to the golden period again. You live in eternal optimism that we can go back to that time and that everything will be all right. We will remind you of those special times that we have spent together and the subtext of doing this will be not lost on you. We are telling you,

"Stay away from us and we will never do these marvellous things again. Is that what you really want?"

We apply guilt and your deep-seated nostalgia for that time. You most likely will have not realised that the golden period was actually an illusion. You will still be mystified at the fact that one day everything was going swimmingly and the next we began to treat you badly. Once again the fixer and healer in you will want to get back to that golden period and now as we unleash this Power Play we are giving you a stark choice.

"Keep this up and never have that again or come back to us."

We are counting on your addiction to the golden period overcoming any reservations and concerns that you may have. We are playing on your fear that you will lose those precious times forever and this is something you will not allow to happen. You may raise our treatment of you and express your concerns and of course we will meet this with sorrow, apologies and another Power Play as we Promise to Change. All that matters is that we use the threatened loss (do you recall that manipulative technique from the devaluation period) of our cherished memories and that the opportunity to replicate them will be lost forever. Is our situation such that our differences cannot be surmounted in order to have those wonderful times again? This is designed to bore deep into your mind and activate the mixture so that you begin to crumble. You decide you want to discuss matters with us but you want assurances. No problem, we will give all the assurances you want, whatever you want to hear and we will even abide by them for a few weeks. We will say anything you want to so long as you come back (submit to our Hoover).

Recognise this Power Play. Understand the golden period was an illusion. There is nothing to go back to and nothing to lose other than your sanity if you allow yourself to be Hoovered. Do not accept this overture. It is but yet another sham and any protestation about how we cannot live without you are purely designed to make you think about what you could lose when in reality you need to focus on what you will gain by maintaining No Contact.

8.17 For the Children

This is a Power Play, which is the preserve of the step-narcissist. The narcissist which you became entangled with is not the biological parent of your children but during the golden period he treated them well, discharged his obligations as good if not great step-parent and managed to worm his way into their affections all part of the smoke screen required to seduce you. Like you, they suffered ay his hands during the devaluation and now, like you, they want nothing more to do with him. He has other ideas instead.

The For the Children Power Play is one where the narcissist will contact you asking about the children.

"It is terrible what has happened between us but I wanted to check that the children are okay."

"No matter what has happened between us we owe it to those beautiful children not to let it affect them. I wondered when I might see them?"

"Even though we are not together I still want to play a part in the children's lives and want to see them. Let's make some arrangements. We can be civil about this."

"I would like to call round tomorrow to wish Tommy Happy Birthday and I have a gift for him. What time should I call around?"

These messages come with the veneer of being kind and caring about the children. If your children still like the narcissist you face a difficult decision. It may upset the children not to see the narcissist any more, especially if his involvement with them was for a decent period of time, but ultimately you must deny the request and reject the attempt at contact for all your sakes.

If it is the case that the children have no desire to see the step narcissist, then your decision is easier. Even though you may feel sorry for us (and of course this is what we are counting on) and you may think that we are behaving in a mature and noble fashion with such sentiments in the messages above it is only a ruse to enable us to get into direct contact with you to continue the Hoover and make you ours again. We have no real interest in the children and in all truth probably disliked them for taking attention away from us when we were with you but we have no hesitation in using them as a device to enable us to get closer to you and effect our Hoover.

Should your narcissist make overtures along these lines you need to recognise that there is no noble sentiment, nothing caring about his intentions. He just wants to use them to get to you and Hoover you. Do not respond to any such messages of this nature that may reach you.

8.18 The False Date

The final power play, which I shall apprise you of, is the False Date. This Power Play requires the use of one of more of my Lieutenants and is used as a fact-finding device to then allow a further Power Play to secure your Hoovering. I will select a Lieutenant who I know that I can rely on and one, which you do not know. His stated brief is to secure a date with you. He may do this by locating you on a dating website if you have signed up for one of those or more likely he will approach you either through social media or in person in order to get to know you with a view to securing a date with you. This Power Play is often used when we do not know where you are but we know you can be contacted. Our Lieutenant will then put in the spadework to achieve a date with you. You may be surprised at how easy this is. I put it down to you needing a distraction from the maelstrom that you have been experiencing and that you regard it as something light-hearted to take your mind off what you have recently experienced.

Once the plant has secured and attended on the date your whereabouts will be relayed to me to allow me to use this for the purposes of a different Power Play as part of the Hoover. We will also use the plant to extract information from you, which we can exploit. He will ask about previous relationships in the anticipation of you mentioning us so we can learn what you are saying about us and address that in an appropriate fashion. In particular, he will be probing for any positive reactions you may reveal about missing us, the traits that you liked in us and so forth so we can maximise those when we are able to secure a face-to-face meeting with you. The Lieutenant will be used as a conduit for information but it will purely in one direction only. He will feed everything he learns from you, to us, so that we can then use it to our advantage.

It will be extremely hard for you to vet anyone you meet to ascertain whether they have a connection to me and at the end of the day this plant will be giving you false information about himself in any event to avoid any chance you work out he is working for me. Accordingly, do not think that you will be able to spot a Lieutenant in this manner. In order to avoid the risk of being picked up in this fashion and information extracted from you, you will need to put in place a no dating policy for a period of time. You may have no difficulty with that since you take the view that the last thing you want is another relationship after what you have endured with us. Nevertheless, I do know of victims, who in order to try and move on or at least enjoy themselves during a difficult period go on dates and they are at risk of being suckered by this Power Play. Enforce a no dating policy for a few months and you will negate this Power Play.

Thus there are the most used Power Plays by our kind and these are what you need to look out for in order to protect yourself and maintain No Contact. These Power Plays will be combined and used over and over again in order to erode your resistance and breach No Contact as part of the Grand Hoover. There are others but these are the most used and also the most effective and therefore these are the ones you must be wary of.

9. What Comes Next?

You implemented No Contact and you have so far successfully maintained it as you weathered the storm that is the Grand Hoover. So what do we have in store for you next? This depends to an extent on the nature of the narcissist you have been involved with and also the duration and intensity of the Grand Hoover.

A Short Grand Hoover Lacking Intensity and a Lesser Narcissist

You got off comparatively lightly. The Lesser Narcissist will not have had the energy or the higher function to go after you with any degree of considerable venom. He will have tried to Hoover because the lure of that Hoover fuel remains delicious to him also. He was not in desperate need of fuel because he clearly had a primary source ready and fully functioning supplementary sources because he did not put up much of a fight to try and win your fuel back. In this scenario the Lesser Narcissist will not have been forced into Chaos Mode but rather he was able to move on to extracting fuel from his new target and leave you alone after a short period of time. He is highly unlikely to come knocking again to seek out Hoover fuel from you unless you present him with an easy opportunity. He will need you to sail very close to him before he will attempt a Hoover. Keep in mind that all of our kind will always look to Hoover because of the reward that us available but some of us will try harder than others. With some of us you need to maintain a greater vigilance post Grand Hoover because we will commit more resources and apply greater endeavour to Hoovering you. However, in this scenario you will only face a Hoover if you move within close proximity to the narcissist. He has his new primary source embedded, he did not experience the Chaos Mode and you will become but a memory unless you choose to go near to him.

A Short Grand Hoover of Intensity with a Greater Narcissist

In this scenario the greater narcissist already had a primary source of fuel lined up and was able to move to it with ease. He had no need to deplete the supplementary sources and therefore the intensity of the Grand Hoover over a short period was all based on punishing you and acquiring the Hoover fuel. It is likely that you will have been subjected to an All Points Broadcast Power Play, which will have revealed that he had moved on to somebody else. Notwithstanding the fact that he will not have faced being pushed into Chaos Mode because fuel was readily available the malign element of the greater narcissist wanted to cause you trouble and pain. He wanted to exact revenge on you for having the audacity to implement No Contact. He also wanted to taste that Hoover fuel. Unlike the lesser narcissist who did not have any malign intent on the agenda, the greater narcissist had and this will remain on his agenda.

In this scenario, following the Grand Hoover, the greater narcissist will make occasional attempts to Hoover you. He will still want that fuel and he will still want to punish you. He will want you back so he can exact a further and more awful devaluation against you after a brief golden period. The only saving grace, if it can be called that, is that he did not suffer a Chaos Period and this will take some of the edge off his desire to grind you into the ground. He will be mainly occupied with his new primary source of fuel but this will not stop him reaching out on occasions and putting some effort into Hoovering you. You should expect an unexpected visit, telephone calls and text messages. There will not be a barrage but on occasions he will recall what you have done and this will unleash perhaps a day of trying to Hoover you before falling silent again for a period and trying again.

Should you make any move, however slight towards him, he will seize on it immediately and look to draw you in.

Accordingly, you will need to maintain vigilance in such a scenario because this greater narcissist will Hoover again and will definitely come after you should you show the slightest interest in him.

A Short Grand Hoover Lacking Intensity with a Greater Narcissist

This will not happen. The short duration will occur because he has fuel from a new primary source and is able to use his supplementary sources effectively. He will not however act with low intensity for the reasons outlined in the scenario above.

A Short Grand Hoover with Intensity with a Lesser Narcissist

In this scenario the lesser narcissist does not have a primary source lined up. This means he will be forced in to Chaos Mode and consequently he will deplete his supplementary sources as he desperately fights to reinstate your supply. He will apply an intense methodology to this but because of his less developed narcissistic instincts and lower functioning as a whole he lacks the energy, discipline and appetite for a sustained campaign against you. He is hoping to obtain a quick fix by blitzkrieging you into submission. He does not have enough energy or appetite to do this for long; it may be a matter of days. Once he realises that he is not succeeding with you then he is obliged, by virtue of the Chaos Mode to break off his pursuit of you and locate a new primary source as he limps along on his supplementary sources. Those sources will now fuel him until he can hook up with a new primary source.

Once he has done so he will then need to repair and replenish his supplementary sources whilst fuelling from the primary source. This period of stabilisation means you will not hear from the narcissist. This may amount to weeks and possibly longer. Thereafter he is unlikely to make any attempt to Hoover you unless you present the golden opportunity to do so. He has learned from his failed Grand Hoover and the significant cost to himself by way of the cessation and draining of fuel that you are a tough nut to crack and he is not equipped to do this. He realises no matter the allure of the Hoover fuel that you might provide that he cannot acquire this unless you present it on a plate to him. He will focus on his new primary source of supply and in this scenario you are unlikely to hear anything again from this narcissist. The only way a Hoover will occur is if you seek him out and ask to come back.

A Long Grand Hoover Lacking Intensity with a Lesser Narcissist

In this instance the lesser narcissist does not have an immediate primary source available to him but he has sufficient reserves from his supplementary sources, which mean he is not forced into Chaos Mode. He no need to apply a sudden short burst to his Hoover in a panicked attempt to break No Contact and Hoover you back. He is neither motivated by malice in a desire to punish you with a sustained and intense attack against you. Instead he is able to cruise along as he hopes to gradually wear down your No Contact defences by repeated Power Plays so that he can reinstate your supply. He is forced to do this as he does not have the primary source in place but he is able to garner enough fuel from supplementary sources to prevent Chaos Mode. He has sufficient fuel to hunt down a new target for a primary source whilst maintaining a slow burning campaign of low intensity against you. He will make attempts to contact you and lure you back in but they will not be amongst the hardest to resist. If you do not crack and allow him to Hoover, you he will eventually find a new primary source of fuel and will then bring the Grand Hoover to an end.

The lure of Hoover fuel will remain an attraction. Furthermore, he has not been forced through the Chaos Mode or a period of stabilisation. This means that he will apply further standard Hoovers from time to time. This is likely to be in the form of an exploratory call or text to find out how you are and to then try a Hoover from that point inwards. There will be no barrages of communications but rather sporadic ones but this will keep happening over a long period of time because he has not been "burned" from the failed Grand Hoover. In such an instance of this you will need to maintain vigilance but as your strength gathers you should find repelling these Hoovers becomes easier. Eventually he will only contact you at times such as birthdays and Christmas with a message, which is sent more in hope than in expectation.

Long Grand Hoover Lacking Intensity with a Greater Narcissist

This scenario will not occur. Whereas above the lesser narcissist was able to sustain a long Grand Hoover even without a primary source of fuel being in place, the Greater Narcissist is unable to do this. This is for several reasons: -

1.   The Greater Narcissist without a primary source of fuel is more likely to be pushed in Chaos Mode and therefore this will increase the intensity.

2.   The Greater Narcissist will deplete his supplementary sources (whereas a lesser narcissist can cruise along more readily relying on them) because the greater narcissist will be consumed with an almighty fury caused by

a.   The criticism inherent in your decision to leave him; and

b.   The absence of the primary source being in place leaving him wrong-footed and again effectively criticised.

The Greater Narcissist will then have such demand on his supplementary sources that he cannot sustain a long period and at the same time his intensity will increase as explained above. Accordingly, this scenario will not take place.

Long Grand Hoover of Intensity with a Lesser Narcissist

This scenario will not happen either because the lesser narcissist will not feel the same level of fury as the greater narcissist. He will not be driven by a desire to destroy your No Contact and you with massive fury. He also lacks the higher function and appetite to achieve this. A Lesser Narcissist will only have a long Grand Hoover of low intensity.

Long Grand Hoover of Intensity with a Greater Narcissist

This is the most dangerous scenario. The Greater Narcissist will act with great intensity owing to his higher function, voracious appetite for your destruction and also his ignited fury at your audacity in going No Contact. He has sufficient supplementary sources to sustain the start of this campaign but he will rapidly deplete them. The Greater Narcissist does not have a primary source of supply in place. He will be fighting however on two fronts. He will be looking to smash your No Contact and Hoover you back in whilst at the same time he is desperately looking for the primary source. He is thrust into Chaos Mode quickly, which causes him to act with huge intensity against you, apply massive effort to secure the new primary source of fuel and also will result in the annihilation of his supplementary sources. Friends will be lost, jobs thrown away, family members cast aside as this whirlwind of chaos goes on the rampage.

If the Greater Narcissist knows the Grand Hoover is failing, he will use the last of his supplementary sources during the Chaos Mode to ensure a new source of primary fuel. Every effort will be made to secure this and this will cause a slight lull in the campaign against you. However, once this new primary source has been put in place, the Greater Narcissist will not enter a period of stabilisation. Driven by hatred, fury and malice he will continue the Grand Hoover now sustained by this primary source. He will go hell for leather to destroy your new contact, Hoover you in and thereafter unleash the mother of all devaluations against you as punishment for putting him through this chaos. Your defences will be severely tested during this period. It will be a frenzied assault as the Grand Hoover moves into weeks. The Greater Narcissist may expend the new primary source and shift to another to keep fuelling his campaign against you. If this is unlikely he will eventually break off his siege because: -

1.   You have not yielded;

2.   The fuel from the primary source has been severely depleted in powering his campaign against you; and

3.   The supplementary sources are most likely exhausted and lost and require replacement.

It is at this point that the Greater Narcissist risks oblivion by using up the last of his fuel to power his fury against you. Accordingly, he will break off to allow himself to replenish the fuel from this primary source since the fury has halted and then re-charged he will seek out new supplementary sources of fuel. This will give you a period of respite as he enters a period of stabilisation. This may take a number of weeks or even months.

Make good use of this lull because this Greater Narcissist has not gone away. Once re-fuelled he will make repeated attempts to Hoover you. They will not be on the scale of the Grand Hoover but he will continue a campaign against you driven by sheer malice. He has his new sources of fuel but this will not matter. You ignited his fury by implementing No Contact, you criticised him, you resisted him and caused him to enter the Chaos Mode, you refused to yield and nearly sent him to oblivion. There is a price on your head and it is Hoover fuel plus your destruction and he will keep at this in the hope of achieving it. In such a scenario as this the repeated Hoover attempts, which will include meeting you, exacting Power Plays again, incessant messages and calls (if those options are available) will go on for years and you will either need to put yourself beyond his reach or maintain a continual vigilance to avoid being Hoovered and the subjected to a terrible and destructive devaluation thereafter.

If you are able to identify that your narcissist is of the Greater or Malign variety and you do not believe they have an alternative primary source available to them, you must be prepared for the very worst when you implement No Contact. In such a case I would seriously suggest that you endeavour to cultivate a situation where you are far from this individual and incapable of being contacted. If not, you will face a hellish Grand Hoover and then you will not be spared his attention in the future as he seeks revenge against you.

Accordingly, you need to have regard to the nature of the narcissist you became entangled with, the duration of the Grand Hoover and the intensity of it, which will provide you with considerable insight into what to expect after the Grand Hoover and what will occur moving into the future. This will allow you to understand what steps you need to take and what you need to prepare for as you maintain No Contact.

It is right to state that when disposing of a narcissist No Contact should be maintained for life. There is no sense, after all your hard work, in doing something, which will expose you to a potential Hoover. The narcissist will make such attempts anyway (on a differing scale of frequency and manner) and there is no reason why you should make it any easier for him or her to do so. You need to remain vigilant but the scale of that vigilance will vary dependent on the scenarios described above. Your strength will return which will assist you in maintaining No Contact but never think you can engage with your narcissist again as "friends" or even from a distance because the mixture remains with you, we know this and we will look to activate it and then Hoover. Unfortunately for you, once you have been involved with a narcissist you always remain at risk of being involved with them again and therefore you need to always maintain your defences. The extent of those defences will vary dependent on the nature of the narcissist but nevertheless they will always need to be maintained. You must always remember that because that delicious, sweet, potent Hoover fuel is something we always want.

Evil

Narcissist: Seduction

Narcissist: Ensnared

Manipulated

Confessions of a Narcissist

More Confessions of a Narcissist

Further Confessions of a Narcissist

From the Mouth of a Narcissist

Escape: How to Beat the Narcissist

Danger: 50 Things You Should Not Do With a Narcissist

Departure Imminent: Preparing for No Contact to beat the Narcissist

Fuel

Chained: The Narcissist's Co-Dependent

A Delinquent Mind

Fury

Beautiful and Barbaric

The Devil's Toolkit

Sex and the Narcissist

Treasured and Tormented

All available on Amazon

Further interaction with H G Tudor

Knowing the Narcissist

@narcissist_me

Facebook

Narcsite.wordpress.com

41402750R10089

Made in the USA
Middletown, DE
12 March 2017